EMERALD HOME LAWYER

GUIDE TO LANDLORD AND TENANT LAW

John McQueen

D1381692

Emerald Guides

© 2018 Straightforward Publishing

British Cataloguing in Publication data. A catalogue record is available for this book from the British Library.

ISBN
978-1-84716-837-5

Printed in the United Kingdom by 4edge www.4edge.co.uk

Cover Design by Bookworks

CONTENTS

Introduction

This Revised Edition of Guide to Landlord and Tenant Law, updated to 2018, is a wide-ranging and comprehensive book dealing with all aspects of the law as it governs the relationship between people and the ownership and tenancy of land.

The relationship between landlord and tenant has always been complex and has changed immeasurably over the centuries, particularly in the 20th century, with the huge social changes that have transformed the structure of the ownership of land. Gradually, the law has provided more and more protection for the tenant, eroding the privileges of the main land owning classes.

This brief book covers the main areas of landlord and tenant law and all of the requisite Acts. The general nature of tenancies is covered, along with the main obligations of landlord and tenant. Repairing obligations are covered as are private tenancies in Scotland. If the reader wants more in depth information about landlord and Tenant law and Housing Rights in Scotland and Northern Ireland then go to:

scotland.shelter.org.uk:

For Northern Ireland, advice can be obtained from www.housingadviceni.org.

The main Housing Acts are covered in depth along with business tenancies and agricultural tenancies, plus Mobile Homes and residential Houseboats. So too is the law concerning service charges and also extension of leases and purchase of freeholds. The chapters are interspersed with relevant case law.

Currently, in 2018, the law concerning leasehold property is under review by the Law Commission as there is the recognition

4

that it is far too complex and open to abuse and is in need of reform.

Although no book covering landlord and tenant law can be totally comprehensive, as the subject area is vast, this particular book attempts to cover the main areas that both the layperson and the student of law need to know.

John McQueen

****

1

An Outline of the Law

The law of landlord and tenant deals with the relationship, or the legal rights and obligations that arise between people when they form a relationship that is connected to land.

Defining estates in land

There are two types of estates in land which are recognised by the law. These are:

1) An estate in fee simple absolute in possession
2) A term of years absolute.

An estate in fee simple absolute in possession

This rather long-winded term means essentially a freehold estate. The holder of fee simple absolute has an unlimited amount of time on the land. This is the closest thing to absolute ownership of land that is allowable under law. The holder of a fee simple absolute is entitled to carve up the land and create smaller estates for fixed periods of time.

A term of years absolute

Under section 1 of the Law of Property Act 1925, a term of years absolute is an estate of fixed duration, i.e. a 125 lease which expires after the duration of this period. A term of years absolute is usually known as a leasehold estate. Whenever a term of years absolute is carved out of a freehold estate the relationship of landlord and tenant arises.

Classes of occupier

Land can be occupied by a person or persons in a number of ways. There are four broad categories of occupation:

- Freehold ownership. As stated, this is where the whole estate is owned indefinitely.
- Tenant. Where a person or persons own an estate for a fixed amount of time
- Licensee. This is where a person is given permission to use the land for a period of time.
- Trespasser. This is where someone simply moves into a premises and occupies illegally.

These are the four categories of occupier at common law. Every occupier falls into one of these categories. When dealing with any type of landlord and tenant problem the first step is to determine to which category of occupier a person(s) belong.

The majority of housing Acts deal with the category of occupier who is a tenant or lessee and not with the other categories, freeholder, licensee or trespasser.

Freehold ownership

The freeholder has the strongest estate in land with the freedom to carve other estates out of it. Witness the great London estates of Grosvenor or Cadogan. Through aristocratic privilege they own great tracts of freehold land in London and have carved other estates in land out of these freeholds. This is the basis of their wealth. However, as we shall see these estates are under attack through the leaseholders right to enfranchise and to extend leases. The occupier who owns the freehold is, in principle, the most secure of all owners with the greatest amount of rights. The estate is unlimited in time; there is no landlord with a superior interest who can reclaim the property or exercise rights over the tenant. There are outside bodies that can exercise power, such a local authorities, with planning powers and compulsory purchase powers. However, on the whole the freeholder is in the most powerful position.

Tenant

The second class of occupier, the tenant or leaseholder has lesser rights than a freeholder but is, nevertheless protected by a strong body of law, the statutory codes, Housing Acts and Landlord and Tenant Acts. For a tenancy to come into existence the following elements must be present:

a) There must be a landlord and tenant
b) There must be exclusive possession;
c) There must be identifiable land
d) The grant must be for a definite period;
e) The lesser must retain a reversion.

The contract of tenancy or lease is usually in writing. A lease exceeding three years must be by deed. Writing is necessary to satisfy section 2 of the Law of Property (Miscellaneous Provisions) Act 1989. Section 2 states:

(1) "A contract for the sale or other disposition of an interest in land can only be made in writing and only by incorporating all the terms which the parties have expressly agreed in one document or, where contracts are exchanged, in each".

For any lease to be created there must be separate legal persons capable of granting and receiving a tenancy. The parties to the tenancy need not be individuals, any 'legal person' such as a corporate entity can grant or receive a tenancy. A tenancy can also be granted to a group of people as joint tenants. A minor, under 18, is not legally entitled to hold an estate in land. Neither is a body which does not in itself have a legal personality. An owner of land cannot grant a tenancy to himself although a director of a company can be a tenant of that company. The company or partnership has a separate legal identity to the tenant.

Where documents are exchanged each party is required to sign his copy for exchange. In Enfield LBC v Arajah (1995) a signature by one of the tenants did not satisfy the requirement under section 2(1) of the 1989 Act. This provision does not apply to a lease not exceeding 3 years, those covered by the 1925 Law of Property Act.

Exclusive possession

This is a fundamental concept. It is fundamental to any tenancy that the tenant must have been granted a sufficient degree of control over the premises for the tenant to be able to lawfully exclude anyone else from those premises, even the freeholder. The tenant will still have exclusive possession if the landlord retains a restricted right to enter the premises for a specific purpose, as is often the case, such as for inspecting the state of repair.

Exclusive possession is an essential requirement for a lease. If the occupier does not have exclusive possession, the right to use the premises does not amount to a lease, although there may be a lesser right to use.

Definition of land

The premises which are the subject matter of the tenancy must be clearly defined.

Term certain

A lease must be granted for a period that is definite. The beginning and the end must be clearly identifiable or capable of being identified. A lease can therefore be for a few days or a thousand years. The most important thing is to be able to identify clearly the term. One such case which highlights this is where a right of occupation held for the duration of the war was held not to be a lease (Lace v Chantler 1944, KB 368).

The duration of a term is not always expressed clearly. There is a distinction, which will be discussed further on, between a fixed term, a specific number of years or months and a periodic tenancy which will run from week to week or month to month and can be determined by notice.

The reversion

For a lease to be created it is essential that the term created is less than that held by the landlord. Although, as we have seen the freeholder can grant a term which is of any length as they have an unlimited duration, a leaseholder can also grant a further lease, as long as it is less than the term of their own lease. Therefore, a leaseholder with a 125 year lease can grant a 124 year lease, the main principle being that it is of a lesser term than the head lease. If the leaseholder sought to grant a lease of 125 years or more then he would have no reversion, i.e. the lease would not revert to him. There would be no rights and obligations outstanding and therefore there would be no relationship of landlord and tenant. The person granted an under lease for the same length of time as the head lease would be in effect assigning his lease.

Rent

Rent as such is not a requirement of a lease. Section 205 of the Law of Property Act 1925 defines a lease as a term of years, 'whether or not at a rent'. One case which highlights this principle is Ashburn Anstalt v Arnold (1988) 2 WLR 706. It was held that an agreement giving an occupier exclusive occupation for a certain term created a tenancy despite the fact that no rent was payable under the agreement. However, it is usual that a rent is paid under a tenancy, particularly periodic tenancies. One famous case which defined the meaning of tenancy was Street v Mountford (1985) AC 809. Whilst rent is not an essential requirement of a tenancy it is essential in order to bring that tenancy within the protection of the Rent Acts.

Types of lease in existence

As we have discussed, the main lease is for a fixed term. At common law, a lease for a fixed period automatically comes to an end when the period expires. No notice is required to determine the lease. there are however, certain statutory modifications to the common law rule relating to residential, business and agricultural leases.

A lease is void if the date of its termination remains uncertain after it has taken effect. It becomes a tenancy at will. It was held in Lace v Chantler (1944) that a lease granted for the duration of the war was void.

Other types of lease, which are not common are leases for life or marriage and tenancies at will and tenancies at sufferance.

Leases for lives or for marriage

A lease can be granted for the life of a lessee. Words which indicate that the lease should be valid so long as the tenant paid the agreed rent were construed in Doe d Warner v Browne (1807) as a lease for life. In Zimbler v Abrahams (1903) the Court of Appeal arrived at the same conclusion. In this case a weekly lease was granted "for as long as the tenant lives and pays the rent regularly". Whether or not the words used in the agreement will give rise to a lease or tenancy for life or for any other term such as until marriage will depend on the construction.

Tenancy at will or at sufferance

A tenancy at will may be created expressly or by implication at any time. It is the lowest estate known to the law. A tenancy at will can arise when a purchaser goes into possession prior to completion, or where a prospective tenant goes into possession prior to negotiations for a lease.

A tenancy at sufferance arises where a tenant, having entered under an agreed tenancy or lease, holds over after the end of the tenancy or lease. A tenancy at sufferance differs from a trespasser in that the tenant entered the land with the consent of the landlord and from a tenant at will in that no express consent has been given. Under section 18 of the Distress for Rent Act 1737, a tenant who holds over under a periodic tenancy and gives notice to quit but fails to give up possession in accordance with the notice will be liable for double the rent whilst in occupation. In such a case, the tenant is not only a trespasser by reason of his notice but will be treated a such by the landlord. A case that illustrates this is Ballard (Kent) Ltd v Oliver Ashworth (Holdings) Ltd (2000).

Tenancy by Estoppel

Once a lease or tenancy is granted, the general rule is that a tenant is estopped from denying his landlord's title and the landlord from denying the tenants title. This rule applies even though the landlords title is defective e.g. where the landlord has been a squatter for less than 12 years. Both parties and their successors in title will be estopped from denying the grant was valid to create the lease or tenancy that it purported to grant, hence the doctrine 'tenancy by estoppel". Therefore the attributes of a true tenancy arises and the covenants contained in any lease are enforceable by the parties.

Owner Occupation

In the strict sense of the term only a freeholder is an owner-occupier as he or she owns the estate in fee simple absolute. Although it is common to term leaseholders as owner-occupiers this is not strictly true as a relationship exists between the freeholder and leaseholder and the freeholder retains a reversion.

Commonhold

The Commonhold and Leasehold Reform Act, an immensely important Act, which we will discuss in more depth later, introduced a new form of occupation, that of Commonhold. It is now possible for a number of occupants of separate flats to own the freehold of their own property right at the outset and also later through creation of Commonhold where leases cease to exist. Although it is possible for a group of leaseholders to purchase a freehold and form a company to manage it, nevertheless they still remain leaseholders, Commonhold creates the situation whereby all flat dwellers are freeholders, or Commonholders.

Commonholders still face restrictions on their rights to occupy parts of property.

Licensees

When an occupier is granted a licence he or she is not given an estate in land but only permission to occupy which can be withdrawn on reasonable notice. The existence of a licence makes a person's presence on the land lawful, as opposed to a trespasser. Licences vary from bare licences where permission is implied, such as friends entering a house or children of adult age staying with you to a more formal licence which, in some cases can be built into a full contract akin to a tenancy. This is known as a contractual licence. Nevertheless it is still a licence and does not imply or impute an estate in land. In the case of bare licences payment can be made but a tenancy is still not created as there was no intention to create legal relations (Hannaford v Selby (1976) 239 EG 811). A fundamental feature of the bare licence is that it can be revoked at any time and the licensee has a reasonable time to leave the premises. Once that period has expired then that person becomes a trespasser. In Robson v Hallett (1967) 2 QB 939 Police Officers knocked on the door of a house. They had no warrant or other authority to enter and were therefore merely implied licensees of the householder. The householder withdrew permission. The court implied into the licence that the officers should be given a reasonable time to leave the premises by the most appropriate route.

One point which has become pertinent is what is the meaning of 'reasonable time'. In the case of family members this can mean as much as six months. (Hannaford v Selby). Where land was occupied under licence for a long period, in this case 26 years, 12 months was seen as a reasonable time (E&L berg Homes Ltd v Gray (1980) 253 EG 473.

Trespassers

A person becomes a trespasser whenever he or she enters the land or premises of another without permission. A burglar is clearly a trespasser. Anyone who does not have permission to be on another's land is a trespasser. From the point of view of a landlord, who, having reserved a right to enter a premises to inspect for disrepair, enters a premises to harass a tenant and interfere with their possessions, the landlord becomes a trespasser if he or she has no right to enter the premises.

Commonly, a trespasser will enter a premises for a short period of time.

Squatters

Section 144 of the Legal Aid, Sentencing and Punishment of Offenders Act 2012 came into effect from 1st September 2012, which effectively prevents squatting of any residential property. Commercial property is unaffected. The penalty for squatting under the Act is £5,000 or six months in prison or both.

The current law, which remains unchanged by the 2012 offence, has several strands and can be summarised as follows:

- Where someone has broken into a property, a criminal offence may have been committed such as criminal damage or burglary. But it may be difficult to prove if there is no evidence of a break in.
- Broadly summarised, section 6 of the Criminal Law Act 1977 makes it a criminal offence to secure entry to a property by force where someone (even a squatter) is there at the time who is opposed to that entry.
- So unless the police are willing to make an arrest, the owner must usually start court proceedings to evict the squatters. Proceedings can take as much as three months to conclude.
- Contrary to popular belief, an exception has existed in one form or another since 1977. Where a "displaced residential occupier" or "protected intending occupier" requests the squatters to leave, the squatters commit a criminal offence by remaining in the property. Since 1995 the law has allowed a displaced residential occupier or protected intending occupier to use force to secure entry, i.e. section 6 does not apply. Broadly, a displaced residential occupier is someone who occupied the property as a residence but has been excluded by squatters and a protected intending occupier is someone who intends to occupy a property as a residence, has a signed certificate to that effect, and is prevented from moving in by squatters.

There is a perception that the current law does not adequately protect property owners, hence the 2012 law. What the 2012 offence does is extend the criminal offence to include all residential properties, not just those that are currently, or about to be, occupied.

The 2012 offence applies where:

- a person enters a property designed or adapted for use as a place to live without the owner's permission,
- the person knows he is doing so without permission, and
- he lives there or intends to live there for any period.

It does not apply where the person has at some point in the past had the owner's permission to be there (i.e. he is holding over after the end of a tenancy or licence).

Where the offence applies, the police have a right to enter and search the property for the purposes of making an arrest where they have reasonable grounds for believing the offence has been committed.

****

2

Obligations in Leases

When a landlord and tenant relationship is created, a series of obligations will arise, usually *express* and *implied* obligations. The promises that are made by landlord and tenant will define a lease and create the relationship between the parties. Many of the express covenants will also be implied so, in cases where they are not expressly stated in the lease, they will seen to be implied, such as covenants for quiet enjoyment and covenants to pay rent.

Express obligations

Obligations and rights in a lease are contractual and these will arise as a result of express agreement between the landlord and tenant.

Express covenants

Covenants are the terms of contract between landlord and tenant. However, a covenant cannot be truly equated to a contractual term as a covenant can continue to impose rights and obligations on people who have acquired an interest in land after the original parties to the agreement have sold up and moved on. In this way, covenants can be said to 'run with the land'.

What distinguishes a covenant from a condition are the consequences that flow from the breach of the covenant.

Express covenants, which will be discussed below, will commonly include:

a) **Landlords covenants**
  1) a covenant for quiet enjoyment
  2) a covenant to repair

17

3) a covenant to insure

4) a covenant allowing the tenant to renew the tenancy or to purchase the landlords interest

Quiet enjoyment

This is usually an express covenant within a lease. However, even if it is not expressly set out in the agreement it will be an implied covenant. All that is required for an implied covenant is that there be a contract between landlord and tenant. A covenant for quiet enjoyment protects the tenant from interference with the most fundamental of his or her rights as a tenant-the right to exclusive possession. Of all the obligations, express or implied it is of the most importance practically in that it covers a number of situations ranging from harassment to disrepair.

One thing a covenant for quiet enjoyment cannot usually do is to provide a remedy for noise pollution. It is a misnomer that quiet enjoyment means noise free enjoyment whereas it does not. It means, essentially, enjoyment without interruption of possession.

However, if noise from a landlord is so excessive that it prevents the tenant's enjoyment of possession it could be deemed a breach of the covenant for quiet enjoyment (Sampson v Hodson-Pressinger (1981) 3 all ER 710).

Acts which amount to interference with quiet enjoyment

Usually it is thought that there has to be some physical interference, for example when a landlord engaged in mining activities underneath a property which caused the house to subside (Markham v Paget 1908)Ch697). Or where a landlord failed to repair a culvert on neighbouring land and as a result water escaped from the culvert and physically damaged the tenants property.(Perera v Vandiyar (1953) 1 WLR 672.

There are other instances of interference with quiet enjoyment. In Kenny v Pren (1963) 1 QB (499) a landlord sent threatening letters and banged on the door of the tenant in addition to shouting physical abuse. This was also held to be a breach of quiet enjoyment. Basically, intimidation is seen to be a breach of the right to quiet enjoyment.

Whether substantial interference has taken place is a question of fact depending on the individual circumstance of the case. Acts which cause inconvenience to tenants but which do not actually disturb their enjoyment will not amount to a breach. For example where the landlord made a noise which merely inconvenienced the tenants privacy (Kelly v Battershell (1949) 2 All ER 830 CA).

Classes of people for whom the landlord is responsible

Acts by the landlord or by the landlords agents or servants or the tenants on the property. The landlord will not be responsible for unlawful acts of persons claiming title under the landlord, for example the tenants. Neither will the landlord be responsible for an act of disturbance by a third party or for a person who has superior title to the landlord, i.e. a head landlord.

Remedies for breach of covenant for quiet enjoyment

An action for breach of covenant for quiet enjoyment is an action for breach of contract and damages will normally be calculated on contractual principles. Contractual damages are usually limited to losses resulting from the breach. A tenant can therefore usually recover damages for inconvenience, for damage to his or her property and the costs of court proceedings.

A covenant to repair

Historically, repairing obligations have been confused and problematic. The basic principle being that in the absence of any covenants to repair then neither party has responsibility. The old principle of caveat emptor will apply, which means buyer beware. The usual situation that arises is that, where there is a written tenancy agreement there will usually be express covenants to repair within the agreement. Also, Landlord and Tenant law places an obligation on landlords to repair and there is a whole raft of case law where landlords have failed to comply with this. The main Act is the Landlord and Tenant Act 1985, section 11 which deals with repairing obligations. In addition to this Act there are other laws, e.g. Gas and Electrical safety which impose a burden upon a landlord.

Usually, the covenant to repair will be constructed in such a way that the landlord will be responsible for the structure and exterior and the tenant for the interior of the demise. In long leases, the landlord will raise monies through service charges either before works (sinking funds) or after works are complete. The 1985 Housing Act as amended by the Commonhold and Leasehold Reform Act 2002 imposes strict obligations on landlords in respect of service charges. The issue of repairing obligations will be discussed at greater length in the next chapter.

A covenant to insure

As it is in the interests of both parties to ensure that a property is safeguarded against fire or other disaster, then there will be an express covenant to insure in a lease. In short leases this is less common because of the short-term interest on the part of the tenant. However, in long leases the landlord will usually covenant to insure the premises with the costs passed on to the leaseholder. A usual problem that arises in this case is where the leaseholder feels that the costs of insurance are excessive. The courts usually uphold the landlords right to insure effectively as opposed to ensuring that the leaseholder receives value for money. However, powers contained within the Landlord and Tenant Acts and latterly the

Leasehold and Commonhold Reform Act 2002 give leaseholders a certain amount of rights when insurance is an issue.

The leaseholder may covenant to insure the premises at their own expense. The landlord may require the leaseholder to insure with a specific company or with a company approved by the landlord. If the covenant states that the landlord must approve the company then the landlord can refuse a company without giving reason (Viscount Tredegar v Harwood (1929) AC 72 HL).

If either the landlord or tenant voluntarily takes out insurance where there is no covenant to do so then there is no obligation to spend the insurance money on reinstating a building. Express covenants to insure normally cover this eventuality and expressly state that monies must be spent on reinstating the building. If the landlord has covenanted with the tenant to insure the building and premiums are collected then, in the absence of an express undertaking to reinstate the building the courts will imply such a term as the insurance was intended to benefit both parties, not only the landlord (Mumford Hotels Ltd v Wheler (1964) Ch 177 (1963) 3 ALL ER 250).

Option to renew lease or purchase landlords interest

Options are different to restrictive covenants in that they give the tenant the right to do something in the future. There are three common rights which the tenant may acquire by way of option:

- An option to renew
- The right to end a tenancy
- The right to purchase the landlords interest in the property

These options will usually take the form of a covenant where the landlord will promise to perform the content of the covenant.

Option to renew

A landlord can, at the start of a fixed term tenancy, choose to give an option to renew the agreement for a further term. This is more common in periodic tenancies than long leases. Long leases are governed by Acts outside of the lease which give leaseholders a body of rights. The right to extend will almost always be with a qualification and this is that the tenant has maintained a well-managed tenancy. A requirement that there be no breach of covenant at the time of the exercise of the option will usually be strictly enforced.

One such example is where a tenant had failed to observe a covenant to repair at regular intervals (West Country Cleaners (Falmouth) Ltd v Saly (1966) 3 ALL ER 210 1 WLR 1485 CA). However, if the breach is not current at the point in time when the tenant wishes to exercise the option the tenant will not be prevented from exercising the right. One court case which highlights this is Bass Holdings Ltd v Morton Music Ltd (1987) 2 ALL ER 1001 CA where the landlord had, in the past, tried to forfeit the lease due to breach of covenant. The court had granted relief and the tenant had complied with all the conditions of relief. In the same year following the breaches the tenant tried to exercise an option to renew. The courts held that, as the breaches were spent the tenant had the right to renew.

Option to determine

An option to end the tenancy (break clause) will usually exist in all tenancies and applies to both parties. The party who wishes to end the tenancy will have to comply strictly with the terms set out in the tenancy.

Option to purchase

An option to purchase gives the tenant the right to buy the landlords interest in the premises at a point in the future. An option to purchase is not regarded as part of a lease but runs collateral to the lease. This option will not usually be expressed in long residential leases but is more common in business leases.

b) Tenants covenants

1) a covenant to pay rent
2) a covenant to pay taxes
3) Various covenants regarding user
4) A covenant prohibiting assignment and/or subletting.

Covenant to pay rent

Although this particular covenant will be either an express or implied covenant, as the relationship between landlord and tenant is almost always for a consideration, the covenant will usually always be express. The amount of rent payable, and the time and method of payments are normally set out in the section of the lease called the 'reddendum'. The reddendum is followed by a list of the tenant's covenants, the first of which is normally a covenant to pay the rent reserved in the redendum. With long residential leases, the rent will usually consist of a ground rent, which will range from a peppercorn, to quite a substantial annual amount. In addition to rent, residential leaseholders will normally pay a maintenance charge (service charge). Service charges do not count as rent and are quite separate. In periodic tenancies, the rent will be higher, a market rent.

Rent review clauses

Leases, in particular tenancies and commercial tenancies will contain a rent review clause which will be effected at a certain point in time. Many commercial leases will specify 5 yearly intervals. The landlord will usually trigger this clause by the serving of a notice. The tenant must then respond within a certain time. Where a rent review clause has provided a timetable by which a landlord should begin the process, problems have arisen where the landlord has missed the due dates. The question that has arisen is whether or not the landlord loses the right to increase the rent after missing the dates laid out in the lease. Basically, the question is 'is time of the essence'? In United Scientific Holdings v Burnley Borough Council (1978) AC 904 (1977) 2 ALL ER 62, the House of Lords overruled earlier authority and held that the general presumption was that time was not of the essence.

Time would be held to be of the essence only if:

a) the terms of the lease expressly provide that time should be of the essence

b) the terms of the lease indicate that time is to be of the essence where the rent review clause is linked to a clause providing an option and that option must be taken up within strict time limits

c) the surrounding circumstances indicate that time should be of the essence.

Certainty of rent

The rent expressed to be payable must be either certain or capable of being calculate with certainty at the date when payment is due. Rent is not always expressed in monetary terms, sometimes t is expressed in terms of services due in kind or in chattels. Courts always look favourably at leases where the rent is expressed as a certainty. However, the intention of the parties is the most important.

An option to renew a lease 'at a rent to be fixed at a price to be determined having regard to the market valuation of the premises at the time of exercising the option' has been held to be sufficiently certain (Brown v Gould (1972) Ch52 (1971) 2 All ER 1505). It can also be sufficient if the parties set out some machinery by means of which the rent can be determined, for example that it should be set by a person nominated by the Royal Institute of Chartered Surveyors. If the machinery set out in the agreement is not clarified or clear, the court may set its own mechanism for setting the rent (Sudbrooke Trading Estate Ltd v Eggleton (1983) 1 AC 444 (1982) 2 All ER 1). However, an option to renew a tenancy which stated that the new tenancy should be 'at a rent as may be agreed between parties in writing' and failed to provide any formula by which the rent could be calculated would not be sufficiently certain (Kings Motors (Oxford) Ltd v Lax (1970) 1 WLR 426).

The tenants covenants for rent should also state the date when the rent is payable. If rent is not paid by midnight on that day then it is held to be in arrears (Dibble v Bowater (1853) 2 E&B 564). Rent may be paid to the landlord or the landlord's agent. If the lease does not specify when the rent is due it becomes payable at the end of each period by which the rent has been calculated. In the case of a weekly tenancy it becomes payable at the end of each week but in the case of a term of years it becomes payable at the end of the year.

New requirements for the payment of ground rent have been introduced by the Commonhold and Leasehold Reform Act 2002. A notice separately demanding ground rent has to be issued. The rent will not be payable until such a notice has been served stating the amount and the date for payment.

In the case of weekly tenancies the tenant can set off rent against any landlords liabilities and this is held to be a defence against cases for possession on the grounds of rent arrears. The tenant must demonstrate that the rent has been put aside and is clearly being withheld because of specific problems.

Recovery of rent
If the tenant fails to pay the rent the landlord has four methods by which he can enforce payment:

1. He can commence court proceedings for the stated rent in the lease (if by deed) or he can sue for the rent stated in the contract (if not by deed) or in the agreement for the lease;

2. he can sue for the use and occupation of the land by the tenant;

3. As an alternative, prior to 6th April 2014, the landlord could have levied for distress in respect of commercial premises; and

4. In addition to the above remedies, he may have aright of forfeiture of the lease, provided that there is a condition for re-entry in the lease.

With effect from 6th April 2014, The Tribunals Courts and Enforcement Act 2007 has abolished distress for rent. It has been replaced by a new regime of Commercial Rent Arrears Recovery (CRAR). Distress which means simple entry and seizing of goods is no longer available. There is now a single fee based procedure which is less draconian.

A covenant to pay taxes
The general rule here is that the tenant pays all taxes due in respect of the occupation. The situation is governed by statute in the case of council tax which is imposed on a person rather than a property (The Local Government Finance Act 1992). In the absence of an express covenant to the contrary it is generally assumed that the tenant is responsible for all taxes.

Covenants regarding user

The general rule at common law is that the tenant may use the premises for any lawful purpose. The doctrine of waste (see next chapter) will prevent the tenant from actively damaging the premises. If the landlord wishes to restrict use or retain any control over the premises then express provisions must be inserted in the lease. Any covenant prohibiting a particular type of user can be absolute or qualified.

Nuisance, damage or annoyance

Many leases will have a variety of different provisions restricting the tenant from committing certain acts. The covenant will be general and will cover any act of nuisance or annoyance committed on the premises. Many periodic tenancies used by local authorities or housing associations will have well worked out clauses whereas longer leases are usually more sparing. Nevertheless it is up to the courts to determine whether or not a nuisance has occurred.

Business use

Covenants may also seek to restrict the use to which the premises are put. Most residential leases will contain a covenant which will prohibit any form of business use. In such cases even partial business use will be a breach of covenant. However, in each case it will be a question of fact as to whether activities constitute business use. A tenant who takes in lodgers on a commercial basis would be in breach of covenant but not a tenant who takes in a lodger who lives with the family as part of that family (Segal Securities Ltd v Thoseby (1963) 1 ALL ER 500 (1963) 1 QB 887). We will be discussing business tenancies further on in the book.

Covenant restricting assignment or sub-letting

In most tenancies there will be an express covenant which seeks to restrict the right to sublet or assign the lease. This effectively prevents the tenant from handing over the lease to another party. The wording of a covenant in the case of sub-letting or assignment is very important. For example a covenant' not to assign' is not breached if a tenant sublets (Russell v Beecham (1924) 1 KB 525 CA). A covenant not to sub let a premises does not restrict a tenant from sub letting part of the premises (Cook v Shoesmith (1951) 1 KB 752). In an attempt to cover all possibilities a landlord will usually draft a covenant requiring the tenant not to ' assign, sub-let or part with possession of the demised premises or any part thereof'. Even this wording might not be adequate if the tenant allows others to use the premises if the tenant is not excluded from the premises. Whether the tenant has or has not given up possession will be a question of fact. Covenants seeking to restrict assigning or sub letting will not prevent a tenant from taking in a lodger.

Absolute and qualified covenants
A covenant against assigning or subletting can be drafted in one of three ways:

1) an absolute covenant against assigning or subletting
2) a covenant prohibiting subletting or assigning without permission of the landlord
3) a covenant not to assign or sublet without landlords consent and that consent not to be unreasonably withheld.

Implied obligations in a lease
Not all obligations in a lease arise directly from express promises made between the landlord and tenant. Covenants can be implied by the common law, which although not expressly set out in the lease are nevertheless implied by common law. These covenants provide the basic minimum of protection for landlord and tenant

where the lease fails to cover basic obligations. Implied covenants include:

Landlord's covenants:

a) a covenant for quiet enjoyment
b) a covenant not to derogate from grant
c) an implied contractual duty of care to keep the common parts in good repair and order.

Tenants covenants

a) a covenant to pay rents
b) a covenant to pay taxes
c) not to assign or sub-let
d) a covenant to allow the landlord entry
e) a covenant not to deny the landlords title
f) a covenant to use the premises in a tenant like manner.

The above are implied in a lease even if not expressly stated.

Covenants implied by statute.

These are the covenants which, although not expressly set out in the agreement will be implied by statute to be part of that contractual agreement. They will augment the minimum standard of protection afforded by the common law.

Obligations arising in tort

These are the obligations based on the principle of a duty of care existing between the parties. These obligations arise independently of contract and so it is not strictly necessary for the parties involved to be in a relationship of landlord and tenant. Tortious obligations can arise either at common law of negligence or nuisance or for breach of a statutory duty.

Usual covenants

These are a particular class of covenants that are implied by the common law into a contract for a lease Where the parties to a lease fail to specify what terms the actual lease should contain, a term will be implied into the contract for the lease that the actual lease when it is granted will contain the ' usual covenants'.

Whether a covenant is a usual covenant or not is a question of fact and may vary depending on the nature of the premises, the purpose of letting and local conveyancing customs. (Flexman v Corbett) 1930 1 Ch 672. However, certain basic covenants will be implied in every case:

Landlord's covenants

- to allow the tenant quiet enjoyment
- not to derogate from grant
- a right of re-entry for non payment of rent
- repairing obligations

Tenants covenants

- to pay rent
- to pay taxes
- not to assign or sub-let
- to keep and deliver up the premises in repair
- to allow the landlord access to view and carry out repairs if the landlord has expressly covenanted to repair
- not to deny the landlord title.

We can see that the usual covenants are in any case usually express covenants or implied.

3

Repairing Obligations

The area of Landlord and tenant law which causes the most contention is that of repairing obligations. Over the years the law regarding repairing responsibilities has tightened up to a degree where any covenants expressed in a lease are superseded by statute.

Caveat emptor

The old doctrine of caveat emptor is still relevant in that, certainly, a buyer should be aware of what he or she is buying. If a person buys a property in bad condition it is certainly going to be expensive to repair. Right at the outset, an in depth survey can save a lot of headaches.

Express agreement to repair

Where a written agreement exists there will, almost certainly, be an express covenant to repair. Parties are free to allocate the responsibility for repairs between them, in a way that they choose. In most cases now the responsibility is split, and is in accordance with the Landlord and Tenant Act 1985 s11. This states that the landlord shall be responsible for the structure and exterior and the tenant shall be responsible for the interior. The length of the lease will be a governing factor. Short term residential tenancies, fixed or periodic, will usually see the landlord responsible for and paying for the exterior and structure and, in most cases, interior repairs too, with some exceptions which we will list later. With a longer lease the landlord will exercise responsibility for the structure and exterior, in order to protect the reversion but the leaseholder will pay for these repairs by the way of service charges (see later).

Construction of repairing covenants

There are a number of ways of expressing a repairing covenant in a lease, depending on what the landlord wants to achieve from a letting. The following are the most common:

To put in repair

This is used where a premises are in disrepair at the outset of the lease and the leaseholder is obligated to bring the building up to a certain standard.

To leave in good repair

This can be expressed in a number of ways, such as to deliver, or yield up, in good repair. This expression is most commonly used and simply means to give the property back to the landlord in good repair, usually in the state that it was in at the commencement of the tenancy.

To keep in good condition

This goes beyond the normal covenant to keep in good repair or that it is imposing an obligation to keep the property in a good condition. Therefore, if a tenant allows a condition to continue, such as dampness and condensation, (Welsh v Greenwich LBC (2000) 49 EG 118 CA) then they are failing to keep the property in good condition.

To keep in repair

This is also a commonly used covenant and imposes an obligation on either tenant or landlord to ensure the premises are kept in good condition throughout the term.

To repair and renew

This is not so commonly used. In essence it does not impose any further obligations on a tenant other than to repair.

To carry out structural repairs

This covenant is usually to be found in longer leases where the burden to pay for repairs falls on the leaseholder.

Structural repairs means repairs to the fabric of the building such as roof, walls and foundations as opposed to repairs to decorations and other cosmetic elements.

It is usually common for the landlord to carry out these repairs with the financial burden placed on the leaseholder. Under periodic tenancies the landlord is responsible for carrying out and paying for structural alterations.

Another repairing term in common use within leases is fair wear and tear excepted. This is a clause most commonly used in short leases. It excludes the tenant from liability to repair damage which occurs due to the natural process of aging. The scope of such a clause is, of necessity, limited and would be limited to the following situations:

If the condition of the premises is abused by use which was not envisaged originally (Bonded Warehouse Co v Carr (1880) 5 CPD 507. If the damage is caused by extraordinary natural events such as earthquakes or floods. Where the cause of the damage can be traced back to a defect which was originally due to fair wear and tear but a consequence of this fair wear and tear has created a situation where the tenant would be responsible for the ensuing repair.

Liability for repairs

An obligation to repair will arise when there is disrepair and the party under an obligation to repair has notification of the defect. For a condition of disrepair to exist two factors must be present:

1) There must be some deterioration of the premises from a previous better condition.
2) The Party responsible must be under an express or implied obligation to repair that part that has deteriorated.

Disrepair cannot be equated with damage. If a house falls into disrepair because, for example, a roof has been leaking into the property then, if no one is covenanted to repair the roof then there is no disrepair. However, one main problem that has arisen here is to do with condensation. Condensation as a form of dampness is distinct from penetrating damp or rising damp. Condensation is usually generated by the occupants, through inadequate heating or ventilation. Water vapour which has been generated through kitchen or bathroom use, or by natural condensation from the human body, condenses on a cold surface and over time will cause damage to the property.

The most striking example of this problem was highlighted in Quick v Taff Ely BC (1985) 3 WLR 98). Severe condensation was caused largely by big metal frame windows. The dampness caused by the condensation caused damage to the tenants furniture, bedding, clothing and decorations. The court agreed that the dampness caused by the condensation made the living conditions of the tenant unbearable but held that the tenant had no remedy against the landlord. The landlord was covenanted to repair only the structure and exterior of the premises. The condensation had caused no damage to structure and exterior.

This finding can be compared to Staves and Staves v Leeds City Council (1992) 29 EG 119 CA) Damp and condensation caused small parts of plaster to perish and the tenant was held able to recover as the structure of the property had been damaged.

Condensation

Condensation dampness is a very significant part of disrepair and has been a source of distress and annoyance for many people. Two further cases highlight the ongoing problem of condensation cases. In Southwark LBC v McIntosh. (2002) 1 EGLR 25 it was held that there is no dispute when a property suffers from damp unless the damp arises from disrepair to the structure and the exterior of the dwelling itself or where the damp has caused damage to the structure or exterior.

In Lee v Leeds City Council (2003) 34 HLR 367 CA the court of appeal affirmed this view. The court, however, also decided that very serious levels of disrepair in a property let by a local authority, caused by condensation, might constitute a breach of the Human Rights Act, right to family and private life under article 8.

Notice of repair

No liability can arise for repair unless a landlord has been notified, either by the tenant or by the landlord's agent or by any other person. To establish liability the tenant must prove that the landlord had advance notification of the problem. The information given to a landlord must be sufficient to have enabled the landlord to take action (O'Brien v Robinson) (1973) AC 912). The complaints must relate to specific items of disrepair

The meaning of 'repair'

One case helped defined the meaning of a repair. In Calthorpe v McOscar (1924) 1 KB 176 CA repair was defined as ' making good damage so as to leave the subject as far as possible as though it had not been damaged.' However, it is really never possible to repair a building and leave it as new.

To repair or renew

When a tenant is granted a lease, particularly a lease of an older property, obviously the components of the house will have aged. If one of the components becomes defective and is replaced with a new component this is renewal. All repair involves renewal and ongoing renewal of components over time will be classed as repair even if the whole building is renewed over time (Luncott v Wakeley and Wheeler (1911) 1KB 905).

The other side of this coin is if a house is deemed to be in such a bad condition that the only course is renewal of the whole. This is clearly not repair. In between, there are many situations where courts have to make decisions between repair and renewal. Each case is considered on its own merit and there is a host of case law considering the distinction.

Inherent defects

As we have seen, basically repair means making good damage to a part of the property. Situations arise however, where inherent defects arise. It is argued that the obligations to repair do not arise when the defect arises from inherent defects in the design or construction of the building. Certain cases have highlighted and supported this view. In Collins v Flynn (1963) 2 ALL ER 1068 a building, due to inadequate foundations collapsed as a result of a structure supporting part of the back and sidewall of a house. It was held that to replace the foundations and replace the structure amounted to an improvement and not a repair.

The doctrine of inherent defect was firmly laid out in Ravenseft Ltd v Davstone Ltd (1980) 1QB 12. Here, stone cladding had become detached from a building due to failure to install expansion joints. The judge in that case found that this was an inherent defect but could be remedied as a repair as the cost of doing so was relatively small. Two other cases highlight the differences between inherent defect and a repair. In Elmcroft Developments Ltd v Tankersley Sawyer (1984) 270 Eg 1289, the original slate damp course in a block of flats had been installed too low, with the result that the lower flats subject to the damp course were damp. To remedy the damp it was necessary to install a new silicone damp course. The courts held that this was repair. The other case, Eyre v McCraken (2000) 80 P&CR 220 CA held that as there was no damp proof course in the building concerned then this was an inherent defect.

Standards of repair

The main case highlighting standards of repairs was that of Proudfoot v Hart (1890) 25 QBD 42. In that case, the judge stated:

'good tenantable repair is such a repair that, having regard to the age, character and locality of the house, would make it reasonably fit for the occupation of a reasonably minded tenant of the class who would be likely to take it'.

Therefore, age, character and location are key factors. Differing properties require different standards, as do differing tenants.

However, over the years various cases have challenged this doctrine as being too rigid. One view which has arisen is that the standard of repair is determined at the beginning rather than the end of the tenancy. Age would obviously be a factor as a tenant cannot possibly be expected to maintain a property as new because of the inevitable aging process.

Common law obligations on landlords

The common law imposes certain obligations to repair on a landlord, despite the general rule that in the absence of an express agreement there is no obligation to repair.

Implied standards of fitness for human habitation
The Housing Health and Safety rating System (HHSRS)

The Housing Health and Safety rating System, or HHSRS, is an official set of procedures for assessing health and safety risks in residential properties.

These procedures were introduced by the Housing Act 2004 and came into force in 2006, replacing the 'fitness for human habitation' rules of the Housing Act 1985.

What is a hazard?

The HHSRS identifies a total of 29 potential hazards that are associated with or arising from:

See overleaf:

Damp/mould growth	Excess heat/cold	Fire
Asbestos	Crowding & space	Radiation
Biocides	Noise	Water supply
Volatile Organic Compounds	Lighting	Explosions
Food safety	Ergonomics	Entrapment
Hygiene	Intruders	Hot surfaces
Lead	Falls	Electricity
Carbon monoxide	Structural issues	Uncombusted fuel gas

What happens when a hazard is discovered?

When a hazard is identified in a property, two tests are applied:

- What is the likelihood of a dangerous event as a result of the hazard?
- If there is a dangerous event, what would be the likely outcome?

The likelihood and the severity of the outcome are combined to produce a 'hazard score'. Hazard scores are divided into 10 bands, with band A being the most serious and band J the least serious. Hazards in bands A – C are called Category 1 hazards and those in band D – J are Category 2 hazards.

If a Local Authority discovers a Category 1 hazard in a property, it has a mandatory duty to take the most appropriate course of action.

If an authority discovers a Category 2 hazard, it has a discretionary power to take action if this is considered appropriate.

This table shows the actions that may be taken by local authorities:

Action	Category 1 Hazards	Category 2 Hazards
Serve an Improvement Notice requiring remedial works	.	.
Make a Prohibition Order, which closes the whole or part of a dwelling or restricts the number or class of permitted occupants	.	.

Serve a suspended Improvement or Prohibition Notice	.	.
Serve a Hazard Awareness Notice	.	.
Take Emergency Remedial Action	.	
Serve an Emergency Prohibition Order	.	
Make a Demolition Order	.	
Declare a Clearance Area	.	.

Landlords who disagree with an assessment may appeal against it by first discussing it with the inspector and if necessary challenging it at the Residential Property Tribunal.

Common parts

Common parts and their upkeep and repair have historically presented a problem to landlords and tenant. There are usually common parts, particularly in large blocks of flats that the tenants have the right to use, but which are separate to the premises leased to the tenant. There may be lifts, staircases, rubbish chutes and so on. Usually, the responsibility for upkeep of the common parts will fall on the landlord with the cost recovered through a service charge. However, sometimes there is no express agreement allocated to maintenance of common parts.

If the tenancy was granted after 15th January 1989 then there is an implied term in an agreement that the landlord has an obligation to repair and maintain common parts. This includes cleanliness and security. This implied obligation is in the 1988 Housing Act s 11(a) as supplemented by the HA 1988 s 116(1). For tenancies granted before this date then there may be a contractual duty of care implied

40

into the contract. In Liverpool City Council v Irwin (1977) AC 239 (1976) ALL ER 39 the tenants of a 15 storey high-rise block rented from the council. There was no proper tenancy agreement only a document entitled 'conditions of tenancy'. This document did not refer to any of the council's obligations. The lifts were out of order due to vandalism and the staircases were poorly lit and also vandalised. The courts considered the situation, specifically the conditions of tenancy. It concluded that, as a matter of necessity a contractual obligation had to be implied into the contract. This imposed a duty of care upon the landlord to maintain common parts.

The contractual duty of care is implied only in certain circumstances. It applies only to the common areas of a building which are within a landlord's control. The term is implied only in circumstances where not to repair would render the contract futile. It is not an absolute duty of care. The landlord need only take a reasonable duty of care. The duty of care only applied to the parties to the contract.

As the common parts are within the landlords control a tenant, or anyone else, does not need to give a landlord notice of repair.

Common law obligations on tenants

In common law a tenant is under a duty to look after a premises in a 'tenant like manner'. This doctrine was laid out by Lord Denning in the case of Warren v keen (1953) 2 ALL ER 1118 at 1121 (1954) QB 15 at 20. In this case, Lord Denning stated:

'The tenant must take proper care of the place, he must, if he is going away for the winter, turn off the water and empty the boiler. he must clean the chimneys, if necessary, and also the windows. He must mend the electric light when it fuses. He must unstop the sink when blocked by his waste. In short, he must do the little jobs around the place that a reasonable tenant would do. In addition, he

41

must, of course, not damage the house, wilfully or negligently and he must see that his family and guests do not damage it. If they do, he must repair it'.

However, Lord Denning also said that 'if the house falls into disrepair through fair wear and tear or through lapse of time, or for any reason not caused by him, the tenant is not liable to repair it'.

Obligation not to commit waste

To commit waste means doing, or failing to do, any act which changes or alters the land. There is voluntary waste where the tenant causes damage to the premises and permissive waste where the premises falls into disrepair because the tenant fails to take action to prevent deterioration.

The extent of the implied obligations imposed on the tenant will vary with the length of the lease. A fixed term lease is liable for both voluntary and permissive waste. A yearly tenant is liable for only voluntary waste with the additional obligation that he or she should keep the premises wind and watertight. However, a yearly tenancy will not be liable for fair wear and tear. A tenant with a shorter periodic tenancy will be liable for only voluntary waste.

Obligation to allow the landlord entry to inspect and repair

This is an implied obligation in the absence of any express agreement.

Covenants implied by statute

In the Landlord and Tenant Act 1985 s 8(1) there are two provisions relating to houses on a low rent and houses on a short lease. On a low rent, there is implied on the part of the landlord:

1) a condition that, at the commencement of the tenancy the premises are fit for human habitation.

2) An undertaking that, during the course of the tenancy the premises will be kept in all respects fit for human habitation.

These terms are implied regardless of any express obligations to the contrary. If the premises are let for more than three years and there is a term placing an obligation upon the tenant to keep in habitable condition s 8 will not apply. 'House' includes flats and bed sits and a tenancy includes all sub tenancies but not a licence. The rent levels in this provision are set so low that the section is now largely irrelevant.

For the majority of tenants on a short tenancy, week-by-week or short fixed term, The landlord and Tenant Act 1985 s (11) will be the repairing covenant. Section 11 applies to any lease of a dwelling house granted after 24th October 1961 for a term of less than seven years. Section 11 does not apply to business tenancies, to tenancies of agricultural holdings or to tenancies granted after 3rd October 1980 by local authorities or to tenancies granted after 3rd October 1980 by the Crown.

The LTA 1985 s 11 states:

1) in a lease to which this section applies...there is implied a covenant by the lessor-

   a) to keep in repair the structure and exterior of the dwelling house (including drains, gutters and external pipes)

   b) to keep in repair and proper working order the installations in the dwelling house for the supply of gas, water, and electricity and for sanitation including basins sinks baths and sanitary

43

conveniences, but not other fixtures and fittings and appliances for making use of gas, water or electricity and:

c) to keep in repair and proper working order the installations in the dwelling house for space heating and heating water.

Section 11 does not impose a duty on a landlord:

a) to carry out works or repairs for which the lessee is liable by virtue of his duty to use the premises in a tenant like manner. S (11) (2) (a). Thus the tenant will still be responsible for performing minor everyday repairs about the house.

b) To rebuild or reinstate the premises in case of destruction or damage by fire, or by tempest or flood or other inevitable accident s (11) (2) (b).

c) To keep in repair or maintain anything which the lessee is entitled to remove from the dwelling house.

Structure and exterior

Over the years a great body of case law has built up regarding the meaning of structure and exterior of a dwelling. 'Structure' in Irvine v Moran (1991) 1 EGLR 261, was held not to include the entire dwelling house but only those elements that gave it its essential appearance, stability and shape. It is important to note that implied covenants only extend to the structure and exterior of the dwelling house concerned, i.e. a third floor flat, and not the whole building although for tenancies granted after 15th January 1989 a new section was introduced into the 1985 HA, s 11(1A) which extended this obligation to the whole of a building in which a lessor has an interest.

Windows are regarded as part of the exterior (Ball and Plummer (1879) 2 TLR 887 CA) and elements such as plasterwork are regarded as part of the structure.

Installations

Section 11 also covers installations for the supply of gas, water and electricity and sanitation and also installations for space heating and heating water. The obligation to keep installations in proper working order may also include remedying design faults that cause subsequent problems of use. For example in Liverpool City Council v Irwin (1977) AC 239 a landlord was obliged to replace cisterns which caused lavatories to overflow. The problem was caused by design. Again, where s 11 did not cover any areas other than a tenants flat, for all tenancies granted after 15th January 1989 the landlord is placed under an obligation to keep in repair and proper working order an installation which serves a dwelling house and either forms any part of the building in which the lessor has an interest or is owned by the lessor and is under his control.

Remedies against a tenant for non-repair

If a landlord has expressly reserved a right of re-entry in a lease or tenancy agreement he may be able to forfeit the lease in the event of disrepair. However, this remedy is now almost impossible under a long lease. It is much easier to achieve under a periodic tenancy. In the case of leases of seven years or more then the landlord also has to comply with the provisions of s 1 of the Leasehold Property (Repairs) Act 1938, of more which below.

Damages

A landlord can seek damages from a court for disrepair which are usually equal to the diminution of the value of the property owing to the disrepair. If a lease of a property has many years to run then the amount recoverable will be less. Therefore the amount of damages recoverable will depend on the un-expired term.

If a landlord brings an action for damages after a tenancy has ended then the amount of damages will depend on the extent of the cost of carrying out the repairs to the property. In this case, the landlord would sue on the basis of the covenant to leave in repair rather than to keep in repair.

Section 18 of the Landlord and Tenant Act 1927 provides the framework for the amount of damages payable to a tenant. It states that damages will not exceed the value of the diminution of the market value of the property due to disrepair. If the market is high at the time then it is possible that the landlord may not be able to recover any money.

Long leases

The Leasehold Property (Repairs) Act 1938 imposes special restrictions upon a landlord. The Act applies to a long lease over seven years and the aim of the Act is to protect a leaseholder against forfeiture mid term because of failure to carry out repairs that may be difficult to remedy.

If a landlord wishes to take action then the Act contains a strict notice procedure, on both sides which has to be observed. The tenant, on receipt of a notice from a landlord, can serve a counter notice and the landlord, if he or she wants to further the action, must prove the following:

1) that the value of the reversion has been substantially diminished by the breach or that the breach must be immediately remedied to prevent the value being diminished.

2) That the breach must be immediately remedied to comply with a by-law, an Act of Parliament, a court order or a requirement of a local authority.

3) That if the tenant is not in occupation of the whole premises the breach must be immediately remedied in the interests of the occupier of the premises or part of the premises.

4) That the breach can be immediately remedied at relatively small expense in comparison with the probable cost of the work is left un-remedied.

5) That there are special circumstances which in the courts opinion are just and equitable to grant leave.

Entering a property to carry out repairs

Where the landlord is under an obligation to repair a property then there will be an implied right to enter. Usually, this is directly expressed in a lease. This provision will also enable the landlord to recover the costs of the work due. This was expressed in the case of Jervis v Harris (1996) 1 ALL ER 303. The amount recoverable is not restricted by section 18 of the LTA 1927.

It is obvious that, when deciding to enter a property, the provisions of the lease must be adhered to. Leases will have a clause, usually, to allow landlords access in emergency if the disrepair is considered such that it is either life threatening or threatening immediate significant damage to the property. If this is the case, and can be demonstrated as such then the landlord is within his or her rights to force entry. In all other cases, reasonable notice must be given and every attempt made to remedy the repair, on the tenant's part, before gaining entry.

Tenants remedies against a non-repairing landlord

The aim of damages in this case is to restore the tenant to a position where they would have been before the problem of disrepair. The damages can be recovered whether the covenant is express or implied. The landlord will only be liable for damages if they have been informed of the disrepair. A reasonable period must be allowed for the landlord to remedy the disrepair. If the tenant refuses to give the landlord access to carry out the repairs then no damages are recoverable (Granada Theatres Ltd v Freehold Investment (Leytonstone) Ltd 1959 Ch 529 (1959) 2 ALL ER 176). The circumstances of the case will determine the damages awarded.

Where a landlord is in breach of repairing covenants the tenant may carry out repairs and then deduct the cost of the repairs from future rent (Lee Parker v Izzet (1971) 3 ALL ER 1099 (1971). Before taking this action the tenant must make sure that the landlord has been notified of the repair and that the repair falls within the scope of the landlords obligations. Withholding of rent on these grounds can be used in a counter-claim for rent arrears.

There are other remedies for disrepair, such as taking out an interim injunction against a landlord, requiring the landlord to do the works. This however, can be costly. It has to be achieved through the Civil Procedure Rules parts 23 and 25 and will usually entail the tenant obtaining a surveyors report. It is only usual to obtain an injunction if the disrepair is significant and it is also threatening the property or the occupants.

Courts may order specific performance of a covenant to repair. A residential tenant may obtain an order requiring specific performance compelling a landlord to fulfil his or her duty.

Appointment of a receiver and appointment of a manager

If a landlord has neglected his duties for years and the tenant sees no point in pursuing the landlord then an application can be made to a court for a receiver to take over the management of the property. The courts will not appoint a receiver to take over management of local authority housing (Parker v Camden Council (1986) CH 162 (1985) 2 ALL ER 141 CA).

Under PT 2 of the Landlord and Tenant Act 1987, as amended by the Housing Act 1996 ss 85 and 86 the tenant may apply to the Leasehold Valuation Tribunal for the appointment of a manager where a landlord persistently fails to maintain a block consisting of two or more flats, Once a notice has been served on a landlord informing him or her of the disrepair and neglect and the landlord has ignored the notice then an application can be made. These provisions do not apply if the landlord is a local authority, resident landlord or the tenant is a business tenant.

Repair notices

Local housing authorities have wide powers over the condition of local housing. These powers are contained within the Housing Act 1985 as supplemented by the Local Government and Housing Act 1989. Notices can be served for a variety of purposes. In addition Environmental Health Departments have significant powers under the Environmental Protection Act 1990.

Negligence and repair

Liability for negligence is based on a duty of care. The duty of care is central to many acts, and, in the case of disrepair if a person or persons, or other entity, fails to take reasonable care through some act or omission and the result is that the other person suffers injury or damage, the injured party can recover damage.

As with other areas of landlord and tenant, the principle of caveat emptor applies. This was illustrated in Robbins v Jones (1863) 15 CB 9NS) 221 at 430:

A landlord who lets a house in a dangerous state is not liable to the tenants customers or guests for accidents happening during the term: for fraud apart, there is no law against letting a tumble down house, and the tenants remedy is upon his contract, if any.

However, society has, thankfully, moved on since then. There are now laws which ensure that a landlord has to maintain a property in good condition.

When is a landlord liable for negligence?

In recent years the law of negligence has expanded to cover all of those involved in the design and construction of the building.

The duty of care extends to common parts also for the acts of third parties. In King v Liverpool city council 91986) 1 WLR 890 the tenant lived in a block of flats owned by the council. A flat above became vacant. The tenant requested that the council secure this flat which it failed to do and it was vandalised and also water flooded out the flat below. The landlord was held liable for the acts of these third parties.

Likewise the landlord is also responsible for any nuisance cause by neglect. Only a person in possession of a premises can sue in nuisance.

There are two main statutory provisions that place a duty of care on a landlord:

Occupiers Liability Act 1957

This provides that:

1) An occupier of a premises owes the same duty 'the common duty of care' to all visitors except in so far as he is free to and does extend, restrict, modify or exclude his duty to any visits or visitors by agreement or otherwise.

2) The common duty of care is a duty to take such care as in all the circumstances of the case is reasonable to se that the visitor will be reasonably safe in using the premises for the purposes for which he is invited or permitted by the occupier to be there.

3) The circumstances relevant for the present purpose include the degree of care, and of want of care, which would ordinarily be looked for in such a visitor so that (for example) in proper cases-

   a) an occupier must be prepared for children to be less careful than adults: and

   b) an occupier may expect that a person, in the exercise of his calling, will appreciate and guard against any special risks ordinarily incident to it, as far as the occupier leaves him free to do so.

The Defective Premises Act 1972

Section 1 of this act imposes a duty on a person or persons who undertake work for, in connection with, the provision of a dwelling:

   a) to do the work in a professional or workmanlike manner
   b) to use proper materials
   c) to ensure with regard to that work that the dwelling will be ft for habitation when completed.

This again applies to all involved in the construction process. However, s 2 of the Act provides that s 1 will not apply to dwellings which are covered by an approved scheme of purchase protection such as NHBC. Section 1 is also restricted by the six year limitation period which begins to run when the building is completed and will only apply to work carried out after commencement of the Act (1 January 1974).

Section 3 of the Act applies to works carried out prior to a sale or letting. It imposes a duty of care in negligence upon anyone carrying out works of construction, repair, maintenance or demolition. The duty is owed to anyone who might reasonably be affected by the defects created and covers tenants, family visitors. The duty also continues to be owed if the property is sold or let.

Section 4 is the most important provision in the Act:
1)where the premises are let under a tenancy which puts on the landlord an obligation to the tenant for the maintenance or repair of the premises, the landlord owes to all persons who might reasonably be expected to be affected by defects in the state of the premises a duty to take such care as is reasonable in all circumstances to see that they are reasonably safe form personal injury or from damage to their property caused by a relevant defect.

The main thrust of lawyers when suing for disrepair hinges on this section. There have been shameful misuses of this section by 'ambulance chasing solicitors' attacking public sector landlords. Nevertheless, it is the most effective provision on which to base a disrepair claim.

Knowledge of the defect
S2 of the Act provides:
2) the said duty is owed if the landlord knows whether as a result of being notified by the tenant or otherwise) or if he ought in all the circumstances to have known of the relevant defect.

The landlord does not have to have actual knowledge of the defect. In Clarke v Taff Ely BC (1984) 10 hLR 44, a tenant was injured when the floor collapsed The tenant had not informed the council of the state of the floor. However, the council was held to be liable for the defect. The house in question and the state of the floorboards should have been inspected.

****

4

Assignments

_____

Assignments and continuing responsibilities

When one person enters into a tenancy with another a contractual relationship is created. Privity of contract is created, which means that the terms of the contract can be enforced against parties to the contract. However, tenancies can be passed on through assignment or another tenancy granted (sublet) which effectively passes on the contractual responsibility to another party. There are rules which determine what happens in these situations.

The Landlord and Tenant (Covenants) Act 1995 changed the rules regarding ongoing responsibilities when assigning or subletting. The Act does not act retrospectively which means that there are two sets of rules governing tenancies prior to the introduction of the 1995 Act, i.e. tenancies granted prior to January 1st 1996 and tenancies granted after that date.

Sub-letting a tenancy

To create a sub-lease the tenant, as we have seen, will grant a term less than the head lease. A sub-lease should normally be granted by deed unless it is granted for a period of less than three years.

Assignment

When a lease is assigned the tenant hands over his or her interest in the property entirely. The original tenant (assignor) retains no reversion and the new tenant (the assignee) takes over the position of the old tenant. However, in certain circumstances this does not mean that the outgoing person ceases to have any obligations.

To ensure that a legal estate is passed on all assignments must be made by deed (LPA 1925 s52(1)). This applies to leases whether created orally, in writing or by deed.

Some assignments are involuntary, such as assignment following death. If a tenant dies then the Administration of Estates Act will govern the vesting of the tenancy in another as part of an estate. Likewise, if bankruptcy occurs then the tenancy will vest in the trustee in bankruptcy.

Tenant's liability after sub-letting or assignment

When sub-letting or assignment occurs, a person who was not parry to the original contract between landlord and tenant has acquired an interest in either part or whole of the property. The question here is to what extent is a person who was party to the original contract still bound by the covenants even though assignment or sub-letting has taken place? Also, to what extent is a person who has acquired an interest bound by the contract?

Under tenancies entered into before 1st January 1996, contractual liability does not end simply because the person who entered into the contract has handed over his interest to a third party. This is because a tenant who entered into a contract prior to 1st January 1996 will expressly covenant to be responsible for the acts and omissions of his successor in title and persons deriving title under the tenant (i.e. sub-tenants). Even in the absence of express terms to this effect they will be implied by s79 of the LPA 1925 unless they have been expressly excluded.

One example is that a party to the original contract will remain liable for the rent due by the new party to the contract for the term of the lease. A Case which highlights this is Estates Gazette v Benjamin Restaurants (1994) 26 EG 140 CA.

This situation can be seen as unjust and the 1995 Act came into being in order to remedy the problem. Under the old Act, the original tenant virtually guarantees the lease and it is up to the tenant to ensure that they pick responsible assignees. The 1995 Act, in addition to changing the position between assignor and landlord, has placed a time limit within which the landlord can pursue the tenant for breach of covenant under leases made prior to 1ˢᵗ January 1996, which is 6 months.

It was even thought that original tenants were liable for breaches of covenants which were variations of the lease made between the new tenant and the landlord. However, one case highlighted this as unjust Friends Provident Life Office v British Railways Board (1996) 1 ALL ER 336.

Statutory restrictions on the common law principles

Though the majority of the provisions in the 1995 Act apply to tenancies post- January 1ˢᵗ 1996 ss17-20 apply to old tenancies as well and offset the consequences of the common law for those who entered into tenancies prior to January 1ˢᵗ 1996:

a) Restriction on liability for rent and service charge. Section 17 imposes a procedure upon a landlord who wishes to recover money from a former tenant. It provides that a former tenant will not be liable to the landlord to pay any fixed charge including both rent and service charge, unless, within six months of that charge being due, the landlord services notice on the former tenant. Effectively, the notice provides a cut-off point after which the landlord cannot recover monies owed.

b) Restriction on liability where tenancy is subsequently varied. Section 18 is included in the 1995 Act where this situation exists It provides that a former tenant will not be liable to pay any amount in respect of a covenant that has been varied.

c) Overriding leases. Once a tenancy has been assigned the main problem encountered by a former tenant is his or her lack of control over subsequent assignees. The 1995 Act enables the original tenant faced with the prospect of being sued, to force the the landlord to grant him or her with an overriding lease. This restores some power to the former tenant by making him or her the assignees immediate landlord. However, an original tenant will only be able to demand an overriding lease where full payment of the original demand had been made to the landlord.

An original tenant who wishes to demand an overriding lease has to do so in writing within 12 months of the landlords demand for payment being made. The landlord has a liability to grant an overriding lease within a reasonable time. The original tenant will be liable for costs.

The new rules

If the tenancy is granted after 1st January 1996 the position is governed by statue as opposed to common law which governs tenancies granted prior to 1st Jan 1996. Section 5 of the 1995 Act gets rid of the principle of Privity of contract. It provides that on assignment of the whole of the premises the tenant will be automatically released from the tenant covenants of the tenancy and will cease to be entitled to the landlords covenants of the tenancy from the date of assignment (s5(2)). If the tenant assigns only part of the premises demised to him or her then the automatic release will only apply to the extent that the covenants fail to be complied with in relation to that part of the demised premises. Where covenants are clearly related to a part of a building that has been demised the tenant will continue to be liable. Where they are not clearly related to a part then the assignor and assignee will be jointly liable. Because of this new system of statutory release it is no longer necessary for a tenant to be deemed to covenant on behalf of himself his successors in title and the persons deriving title under him nor for an implied indemnity covenant to be inserted into the lease.

Authorised guarantee agreements

The 1995 Act has introduced a mechanism which goes some way towards protecting landlords as they now no longer have any say in selecting assignees after 1st Jan 1996. The authorised guarantee agreement requires in certain circumstances, that a tenant remains contractually liable after assignment. The landlord can require this in the following circumstances:

a) the agreement must be one under which the tenant guarantees the performance of the covenant by the assignee (s16(2) (a))

b) there must be a covenant against assignment in the lease which prevents the tenant from effecting the assignment without the consent of the landlord (s16 (3)(a):

c) the assignment of a lease is subject to a condition that requires the tenant to enter into an agreement guaranteeing the performance of the covenant by the assignee (s16(3)(c)

The scope of the authorised agreement is limited by statute. It must not impose on the tenant any requirement to guarantee in any way the performance of the relevant covenant by any other than the immediate assignee and it must not impose on the tenant any liability restriction or requirement of whatever nature in relation to any time after the assignee is released from that covenant by virtue of the 1995 Act. Thus the immediate tenant will be required to guarantee the immediate assignee.

Excluded assignments
The release of landlord and tenant covenants will not apply in the case of an excluded assignment. There are two types of excluded assignment:

a) assignments in breach of a covenant in a tenancy, for example where the agreement contains a covenant forbidding assignment;

b) assignments by operation of law such as death or bankruptcy.

Where a landlord or tenant remains bound because the assignment made was an excluded assignment he or she will nevertheless be released if and when a further assignment of the tenancy is made provided that the further assignment is not an excluded assignment.

Liability between persons not party to the original agreement
In relation to the person who acquires an interest in land, under the old rules the situation is governed by the rule in Spencers Case (1583) 5 Co

Rep 16a. The rule states that the assignee of a tenancy will acquire both the burden and the benefits of the covenants in a lease provided that:

a) there is privity of estate between the person seeking to enforce the covenant and the person against whom he is seeking to enforce it;

b) the covenant in question touches and concerns the land.

Privity of estate

This arises when two parties are in a relationship of landlord and tenant. There will be privity of estate between parties regardless of whether the parties have contracted with each other.

Covenants that touch and concern the land

A covenant will 'touch and concern the land' if it affects landlord and tenant. One such case that highlighted this was Breams Property Investment Co Ltd v Stroulger (1948) 2 KB 1.

Virtually all of the common covenants considered so far in this book touch the land. Covenants concerning rent and repair, user and quiet enjoyment will certainly touch the land. Although the number of covenants can be unlimited the following covenants have been held to touch the land:

a) A covenant requiring the tenant to sell only a landlords brand of product on the premises Clegg v Hands (1890) 44 ChD 503.

b) A covenant requiring a tenant not to permit a particular person to be involved with the running of the business on the premises (Lewin v American and Colonial Distributors Ltd (1945) Ch 255 1 ALL ER 529.

A covenant will not touch the land if it does not concern the landlord and tenant in their capacity as landlord and tenant or of it does not directly reference the land. Such covenants have been held to be the option to buy the premises or an entitlement to put up advertising.

Liability after assignment under the new rules

For new tenancies, as we have seen, the situation is governed by statute. Section 3 of the 1995 Act provides:

(1) The benefit and burden of all landlord and tenant covenants of a tenancy-

a) shall be annexed and incident to the whole and to each and every part of the premises demised by the tenancy and the reversion in them, and

b) shall in accordance with this section pass on assignment of the whole or any part of the whole premises or the reversion in them.

Thus section 3 fixes the benefits and burdens of all covenants to the land. There is no need to consider whether the covenant in question touches and concerns the land. In addition, where a tenant assigns his or her tenancy the assignee will become bound by the tenants covenants in the tenancy and entitled to the benefits of the landlord covenants in the tenancy. The provisions contain a number of exceptions. First the assignee will not be bound by tenant covenants that immediately before the assignment did not bind the assignor.

Liability of the assignor to the assignee

Where an assignment was made before 1st July 1994 the Law of Property Act 1925 s76 implies a number of covenants into the transaction on the part of the assignor for the benefit of the assignee. These are: covenants for title; a covenant for quiet enjoyment; a covenant for further assurance and a covenant that the lease is not liable to forfeiture and that the tenants covenants have been performed by the assignor.

Where the assignment was made after July 1st 1994, Part 1 of the Law of Property Act (Miscellaneous Provisions) 1994 will apply to the transaction. Again, these provisions imply covenants on the part of the assignor that he or she has good title, and in the case of leasehold land that the lease is subsisting at the date of disposition and that there is no breach of the tenants obligation and that the lease is not liable to forfeiture.

Liability of the assignee to the assignor

Assignments made prior to the coming into force of the Landlord and Tenant (covenants) Act 1995 will contain an implied covenant on the part of the assignee that he or she would, at all times from the date of the assignment, pay the rent and perform the tenants covenants and indemnify the assignor against failure to do so. Where the assignment was made after 1st January 1996 the exclusion of continuing liability afforded to the tenant by the 1995 Act means that this implied covenant is no longer necessary.

Liability after the sale of the landlords interest in the property

In the case of tenancies entered into before 1st January 1996 the question as to whether the benefit and burden of the covenants in the original lease will run to bind an assignee of the reversion is determined by statute. Section 141 of the LPA 1925 states that 'the rent reserved by a lease and the benefits of all the covenants in a lease which refer to the subject matter in the lease' will run to benefit the assignee of the conversion. In addition the obligations will run to bind an assignee.

Liability after the sale of the reversion under the new rules

For new tenancies the rules which govern the transmission of the benefit and burden of the covenants contained in the original lease after the assignment of the reversion are almost identical to those which govern transmission when there is an assignment of the tenancy. An assignee of the landlords reversion will be bound by the landlords covenants in the tenancy and becomes entitled to the benefit of the tenants covenants.

Liability of sub-lessees

Under the old rules the relationship is between the landlord and the lessee in a contractual relationship of privity of contract. The sub-lessee is in a contractual relationship with the lessee. The covenants in a head tenancy will not run to bind a sub-lessee. There is one exception. A head lessee may be able to enforce a covenant in the head tenancy against a sub-lessee under the rule in Tulk v Moxhay (1848) 2 Ph 774. This rule allows the head landlord to enforce a restrictive covenant against any occupier who takes possession of the premises with notice of the covenant. A restrictive covenant can be registered as a minor interest in registered land or as a class D(ii) land charge in unregistered land. If the restrictive covenant is registered the occupier will be deemed to have notice of that covenant even if they have no knowledge of it.

Under the new rules

The provisions of the 1995 Act do not apply to the transmission of the burdens and benefits of covenants on assignment. They do not function to make covenants enforceable between a head landlord and a sub-tenant.

****

5

The Rent Act 1977-The Protected Tenant

If a tenancy agreement was granted before 15th January 1989 then, in most cases, it will be a Rent Act protected agreement. However, there are a number of exceptions to this and they are listed further on in this chapter.

Most tenancies are now assured tenancies. However, despite this, there are still a (very) small number of older Rent Act protected tenancies in existence.

What Rent Act protection means is that the rules which guide the conduct of the landlord and tenant are laid down in the Rent Act 1977.

This Act was passed to give tenants more security in their home. It is called a Rent Act because its main purpose is to regulate rents, but the Act also gives tenants other rights such as protection from eviction.

It is mainly only tenants who can enjoy protection under the Rent Act of 1977, not usually licensees or trespassers who have limited rights. A tenancy will be protected provided that the landlord does not live on the premises. If a landlord lives in the same accommodation as the tenant then the tenant will not be protected by the 1977 Rent Act. To live in the same premises means to share the same flat as the tenant and not, for example, to live in the same block of flats.

In addition, Rent Act protection means that the rent will be regulated This basically means that the tenant has the right to a fair rent set by a Rent Officer employed by the local authority.

The fair rent is set every two years and the landlord is not free to charge as he or she wishes. Once set the rent cannot be altered.

Rent Act protection also means protection from eviction which means that the landlord is not free to evict.

For a tenancy to be protected, however, the tenant must be using the property as his/her main residence. If they are not, and the fact can be proved, then they will lose protection and the landlord can evict with less trouble.

SECURITY: THE WAYS IN WHICH THE TENANT CAN LOSE HIS/HER HOME AS A PROTECTED TENANT

When a tenant signs a tenancy agreement he or she is signing a contract where both landlord and tenant are agreeing to accept certain rights and responsibilities.

In the agreement, there are a number of grounds for possession which enable the landlord to recover his or her property if the contract is broken by the tenant, e.g., by not paying the rent. These may not always be referred to in the agreement but this can be found in the 1977 Rent Act.

If a landlord wishes to take back his or her property he/she must serve the tenant with a notice to quit (the premises) which must give twenty eight days notice of intention to seek possession of the property (to begin to recover the property) and, following the expiry of the twenty eight days an application must be made to court to repossess the property.

When the landlord serves the notice to quit the reasons for his doing so should be stated in a covering letter to the tenant and should be based on the grounds for possession outlined in the agreement.

A landlord cannot simply evict a tenant, or use menaces (harassment) to do so. There is protection (Protection from Eviction Act 1977) and the landlord must apply to court to get a tenant out once the twenty eight days have expired.

When a landlord has served a notice to quit, a tenancy becomes a "statutory tenancy" which exists until a court order brings it to an end. Briefly, the reasons for a landlord wanting possession will be based on one of ten mandatory or ten discretionary grounds for possession.

Mandatory grounds for possession means that the court must give the landlord possession of the property, which means that the judge has no choice in the matter.

Discretionary grounds for possession means that the court can exercise some discretion in the matter (i.e. can decide whether or not to order eviction) and it is up to the landlord to prove that he is being reasonable. Discretionary grounds usually correspond to the tenants obligations in the tenancy.

It is very rare, in the first instance, if the grounds are discretionary, for a landlord to gain possession of a property unless it is obviously abandoned or the circumstances are so dramatic. Usually a suspended order will be granted.

A suspended order means that the tenant will be given a period of time within which to solve the problem, i.e come to an agreement with the landlord. This time period is, normally, twenty eight days. So, for example, if a tenant has broken an agreement to pay the rent, the judge may give twenty eight days in which either to pay the full amount or to reach an agreement with the landlord.

Listed below are the grounds for possession which can be used against a tenant by a landlord. Full details of all grounds can be found in the 1977 Rent Act

The discretionary grounds for possession of property covered by the 1977 Rent Act

Ground One is where the tenant has not paid his or her rent or has broken some other condition of the tenancy.

Ground One covers any other condition of the tenancy. This includes noise nuisance, unreasonable behaviour and, usually, racial or sexual harassment.

Ground Two is where the tenant is using the premises for immoral or illegal purposes, eg, selling drugs, prostitution. It also covers nuisance and annoyance to neighbours.

Grounds Three and Four are connected with deterioration of the premises as a direct result of misuse by the tenant.

Ground Five is that the landlord has arranged to sell or let the property because the tenant gave notice that he was giving up the tenancy.

Ground Six arises when the tenant has sub-let the premises, ie, has created another tenancy and is no longer the only tenant. Usually, the landlord will prohibit any sub-letting of a flat.

Ground Seven no longer exists.

Ground Eight is that the tenant was an employee of the landlord and the landlord requires the property for a new employee.

Ground Nine is where the landlord needs the property for himself or certain members of his family to live in.

Ground Ten is that a tenant has charged a subtenant more than the Rent Act permits.

One other important discretionary ground does not appear in the list of grounds in the 1977 Rent Act. It relates to the provision of suitable alternative accommodation. If the landlord requires possession of the property for reasons such as carrying out building works then it must be demonstrated that suitable alternative accommodation can be provided by the landlord for the tenant.

The mandatory grounds for possession of a property

These are grounds on which the court must give possession of a property to the landlord. The judge has no choice in the matter. If such an order is granted then it cannot be postponed for more than fourteen days, except where it would cause exceptional hardship when the maximum is six weeks. There are two basic rules for using the mandatory grounds:

1. The landlord must give a written notice saying that he/she may in future apply for possession under the appropriate ground. He/she must give it to the tenant normally when or before the tenancy begins (before the tenancy was granted, in the case of shorthold) and;
2. When he/she needs possession, the conditions of the appropriate ground must be met.

The mandatory grounds are as follows:

Ground Eleven. This ground is available only when the landlord has served notice at the beginning of the tenancy stating when he or she wants back the premises, ie, a date is specified.

Ground Twelve is valid only when a landlord has served notice that the property may be required for personal use as a retirement home. Ground Thirteen applies only where the letting is for a fixed term of not more than eight months and it can be proved that the property was used as a holiday letting for twelve months before the letting began.

Ground Fourteen is that the accommodation was let for a fixed term of a year or less, having been let to students by a specified educational institution or body at some time during the previous twelve months.

Ground Fifteen is that the accommodation was intended for a clergyman and has been let temporarily to an ordinary client.

Ground Sixteen is that the accommodation was occupied by a farmworker and has been let temporarily to an ordinary tenant.

Ground Seventeen-Farmhouses made redundant by amalgamation. Under this ground a dwelling house was originally occupied by a person responsible for farming land but the dwelling house has been made redundant under a scheme of amalgamation under the Agriculture Act 1967. The landlord can recover possession of the property if it is again required for a person employed in agriculture.

Ground Eighteen-farmhouses made redundant without amalgamation. This ground applies where a dwelling houses was formerly occupied by someone responsible for farming the land where the dwelling is situated. At that time the dwelling was subject to a regulated tenancy and the tenant was served with prior written notice that possession might be recovered under this ground.

Ground Nineteen-Protected Shorthold Tenancy. This type of tenancy preceded the assured shorthold tenancy and was created under the Housing Act 1980 which permitted the landlord to grant a short fixed term tenancy of between one and five years without the benefit of security of tenure to the tenant. Such a tenancy was phased out of existence after 15th January 1989.

Ground Twenty-Armed Forces Personnel-this is a ground which is similar to grounds 11 and 12. Ground 20 enables a member of the armed forces to purchase a property and rent it out with the intention of occupying at some time in the future when recovery of possession is needed.

PRIVATE SECTOR AGREEMENTS SIGNED BEFORE JANUARY 1989 BUT WHICH DO NOT HAVE RENT ACT PROTECTION:

Not all people who entered into agreements before 15th January 1989 will be protected tenants under the 1977 Rent Act.

The licence

Private landlords had proved unwilling to accept protected tenants as it meant that tenants would have the right to a low rent and would be difficult to get out. As a result, landlords devised a number of loopholes which enabled them to avoid granting a protected tenancy. One such arrangement was the licence agreement. A licence is a personal arrangement between the landlord (licensor) and the licensee. The main difference between a licensee and a tenant is that the licensee, right from the beginning, has far less security than a tenant.

A licence to occupy a house, or part of a house, is the same, in principle, as a licence to drive a car or to run a public house. It gives permission to stay which is temporary and can be withdrawn. Landlords found licences attractive because the protection which was given to tenants by the 1977 Rent Act and the 1988 Housing Act was not given to the licensee.

This meant that the landlord could evict the licensee, without giving twenty eight days notice and without getting a court order. Or at least this seemed to be the case. Hardly surprising, then, that licences were so popular with landlords.

However, with the advent of the Assured Shorthold Tenancy and the changes in definition of 'licence' agreement' particularly following the case of Street v Mountford, licences are no longer used except in specific circumstances.

Other agreements signed before 1989 which are not protected

There are other types of agreement which will not be classed as a protected tenancy.

Tenancies granted before 14th August 1974, and which are furnished with a resident landlord

If a tenancy was entered into before the above date and the property was furnished to a reasonable standard it is not considered to be protected. This is another complex area and no longer really relevant with the passage of time, and will not be pursued further here.

Restricted contracts under the 1977 Rent Act

A tenancy entered into before 15th January 1989 will not be protected if, when the tenancy was first entered into, the landlord was still living in the same building as the property which has been let to the tenant. This is known as a restricted contract. The exception is the situation where the block is purpose-built and the landlord has a separate flat.

However, if one landlord sells his interest to another person who intends to live in the building, the tenancy will remain unprotected for twenty eight days. In that twenty eight days the person taking over the property can either take up residence or serve written notice that he intends to do so within the next six months.

As long as he/she takes up residence within six months the notice serves to prevent the tenancy becoming protected.

If a tenancy is not protected because it falls within the above category then it is known as a restricted contract. However, one important point is that a restricted contract will cease to be such after the passing of the 1988 Rent Act when there is a change in the amount of rent payable under the contract other than a change determined by the rent tribunal.

From then on, the restricted contract becomes an assured tenancy. More about assured tenancies later.

Flats and houses under certain rateable values

If the property had a specific rateable value that property could be the subject of a protected tenancy. In practice, few properties are above this figure.

Tenancies at low rents

A tenancy which was entered into before 1st April 1990 is not a protected tenancy if the rent paid is less than two-thirds of the rateable value of the property on the appropriate day. The appropriate day is 23rd March 1973 unless the property was valued at a later date. If no rent is paid then the tenancy will not be protected.

Flats and houses let with other land

If a property was let with other land to which it was only an adjunct (an addition) then it would not be a protected tenancy. However, importantly, unless the other land consisted of more than two acres of agricultural land, it would be taken as part of the dwelling house and would not prevent the tenancy being protected.

Payments for board and attendance

If a part of the rent for which a house is let was payable in respect of board or attendance there would not be a protected tenancy. Board, which is the provision of meals, must have been more than minimal if the tenancy was not to be protected.

Provision of a continental breakfast would be enough, whilst the provision of hot drinks would not. Attendance included personal services such as making beds. This provision is one that was often used by landlords to avoid the Rent Act. Such a tenancy, though, may form a restricted contract (see above).

Lettings to students

A tenancy granted by a specified educational institution to students studying will not be protected (the institution will usually be a university or college of further education).

Holiday lettings

A tenancy is not a protected tenancy if its purpose is to give the tenant the right to occupy the dwelling for a holiday.

Agricultural holdings

A tenancy is not protected if the dwelling is part of an agricultural holding and is occupied by the person responsible for the control of the farming of the holding. Tenancies of this sort are subject to the control of the Agricultural Holdings Act 1986 and other areas of the law.

Licensed premises

Where a tenancy of a dwelling house consists of or comprises premises licensed for the sales of alcohol, there will not be a protected tenancy.

Resident landlords

The tenancy will not be protected if, at the commencement of the tenancy, the landlord was resident in the same building as the property which has been let. This does not apply if the landlord merely has another flat in a purpose-built block; he must be in the same building or residence.

Where the landlord is a local authority, the Crown, a housing - association or a co-operative

The tenancy will not be protected where the landlord is one of the above. Tenants of local authorities, housing associations, the Crown or a Co-operative have a different sort of protection, which this guide does not go into.

Company lets

Only an individual person is capable of living in a flat or house. If a property is let to a company there can be no statutory (legal) tenancy. When a property is let to a company, the tenancy would be between that company and a landlord. There are certain circumstances, however, where a company let can be a protected tenancy and the fair rent legislation applies.

6

PUBLIC SECTOR TENANCIES

Renting from a social housing landlord
Who is a tenant of a social housing landlord

You are a tenant of a social housing landlord if you are a tenant of:

- a local authority. These are district councils and London borough councils; or
- a housing association; or
- a housing co-operative.

Local authority tenants

If you are a tenant of a local authority you are likely to be a secure tenant or an introductory tenant. In England, from 1 April 2012, local authorities can also grant flexible tenancies.

Housing association and housing co-operative tenants
Tenancy began before 15 January 1989

If you are a housing association or housing co-operative tenant and your tenancy began before 15 January 1989, you will be a secure tenant. For details about the rights a secure tenant has, see below.

Tenancy began on or after 15 January 1989

If you are a housing association or housing co-operative tenant and your tenancy began on or after 15 January 1989, you are likely to be an assured tenant. Some association tenants may be starter tenants for the first 12 to 18 months. A starter tenancy is a type of assured shorthold tenancy.

In England, from 1 April 2012, housing associations can use assured shorthold tenancies for tenancies other than starter tenancies.

Rights of secure tenants

As a secure tenant you have the right to stay in the accommodation unless your landlord can convince the court that there are special reasons to evict you, for example, you have rent arrears, damaged property or broken some other term of the agreement. As well as the right to stay in your home as long as you keep to the terms of the tenancy, you will also have other rights by law: These include the right:

- to have certain repairs carried out by your landlord
- to carry out certain repairs and to do improvements yourself - see under heading Repairs and improvements
- to sublet part of your home with your landlord's permission
- to take in lodgers without your landlord's permission
- to exchange your home with certain other social housing tenants
- if you are a local authority tenant, the right to vote to transfer to another landlord
- to be kept informed about things relating to your tenancy
- to buy your home.
- if you are a housing association tenant whose tenancy started before 15 January 1989, the right to a 'fair rent' - see under heading Fixing and increasing the rent
- for your spouse, civil partner, other partner or in some cases a resident member of your family, to take over the tenancy on your death (the right of 'succession')

- to assign (pass on) the tenancy to a person who has the right of 'succession' to the tenancy. This is sometimes difficult to enforce
- if you are a local authority tenant, to take over the management of the estate with other tenants by setting up a Tenant Management Organisation not to be discriminated against because of your disability, gender reassignment, pregnancy and maternity, race, religion or belief, sex or sexual orientation.

You will usually have a written tenancy agreement which may give you more rights than those set out above.

Complaints about secure tenancies

Each social housing landlord must have a clear policy and procedure on dealing with complaints. You should have the opportunity to complain in a range of ways. If after using your landlord's complaints procedure you are still dissatisfied, you can complain to an Ombudsman about certain problems. In England, if you are a local authority tenant this will be the Local Government Ombudsman, and if you are a housing association tenant it will be the Housing Ombudsman. If you have suffered discrimination, you can complain about this to the Ombudsman. In Wales, you can complain to the Public Services Ombudsman for Wales.

Rights of assured tenants

As an assured tenant you have the right to stay in your accommodation unless your landlord can convince the court there are reasons to evict you, for example, that there are rent arrears, damage to the property, or that another of the terms of the agreement has been broken.

As an assured tenant you can enforce your rights, for example, to get repairs done, without worrying about getting evicted. As well as the right to stay in your home as long as you keep to the terms of the tenancy you will also have other rights by law including:-

- the right to have the accommodation kept in a reasonable state of repair

- the right to carry out minor repairs yourself and to receive payment for these from your landlord - see under heading Repairs and improvements

- the right for your spouse, civil partner or other partner to take over the tenancy on your death (the right of 'succession')

- the right not to be treated unfairly by your landlord because of your disability, gender reassignment, pregnancy and maternity, race, religion or belief, sex or sexuality.

You will usually have a written tenancy agreement which may give you more rights than those set out above.

Complaints about assured tenancies

Each housing association must have a clear policy and procedure on dealing with complaints. You should have the opportunity to complain in a range of ways. If after using your landlord's complaints procedure you are still dissatisfied, you can complain in England, to the Housing Ombudsman, or in Wales, to the Public Services Ombudsman for Wales.

Starter tenancies and assured shorthold tenancies

A starter tenancy is the name often used by housing associations to describe an assured shorthold tenancy. Starter tenancies are probationary tenancies which allow a landlord to evict you more easily if you break the terms of your tenancy agreement.

A starter tenancy generally lasts for 12 months, although they can be extended to 18 months. As long as no action has been taken by the landlord to end the tenancy within the starter period, the starter tenant can then become an assured or longer-term assured shorthold tenant in England, or an assured tenant in Wales.

In England, housing associations can use assured shorthold tenancies for tenancies other than starter tenancies. They are likely to last for a fixed term of five years or more, but in some cases will last for two years. These tenancies may also be on 'affordable rent' terms.

In England, if you have an assured shorthold tenancy of a fixed term of two years or more with a housing association landlord, you will generally have similar rights to an assured tenant. However, if you have a fixed term tenancy, you only have the right to stay in your home for the length of the fixed term.

Complaints about starter and assured shorthold tenancies

Each housing association must have a clear policy and procedure on dealing with complaints. You should have the opportunity to complain in a range of ways. If after using your landlord's complaints procedure you are still dissatisfied, you can complain in England, to the Housing Ombudsman, or in Wales, to the Public Services Ombudsman for Wales.

Fixing and increasing the rent
Local authority tenancies

Rents for local authority tenants are fixed according to the local authority's housing policy and the amount of money they get from central government. You cannot control the amount of rent payable, but may be able to claim housing benefit to help pay it.

Housing association and housing co-operative tenancies which began before 15 January 1989

If you are a housing association or housing co-operative tenant whose tenancy started before 15 January 1989 you are a secure tenant, but your rent is generally a 'fair rent' registered by the Rent Officer. The housing association or co-operative will usually have had the rent registered.

Once a rent has been registered, a new rent cannot usually be considered for the accommodation for two years. The rent can only be increased if:-

- you ask for a new fair rent assessment after two years

- your landlord asks for a new fair rent assessment after one year and nine months, although any new rent would not become effective until the end of two years.

An application for a rent increase can be made earlier, but only if the tenancy has changed drastically or if you and your landlord apply together. If you need help paying the rent you may be able to claim housing benefit.

Assured tenants
Housing association or housing co-operative tenancies which began on or after 15 January 1989

Many housing association tenants whose tenancy started on or after 15 January 1989 are assured tenants. If you are an assured tenant, your rent is the rent you agreed to pay your landlord at the beginning of the tenancy and should be covered in your tenancy agreement. The tenancy agreement should also state when and how the rent can be increased.

In England, most housing associations and housing co-operatives are registered with the Homes and Communities Agency and must follow standards and procedures set down by this regulatory body. They are sometimes known as social landlords. They set rents in accordance with government guidance and tenants have to be given clear information about how their rent and service charges are set and how they can be changed.

You may have the right to apply to a Rent Assessment Committee if you do not agree to a rent increase.

In Wales, housing associations must manage their housing to standards set by the Welsh Government. You must be informed in writing, and in advance about any changes in your rent. You should be given at least 28 days notice of any increase. You may have the right to apply to a Rent Assessment Committee if you do not agree to a rent increase.

If you are a housing association tenant in Wales, there is a leaflet explaining your rights called The Guarantee for Housing Association

Residents. You can find this on the Welsh Government website at: www.new.wales.gov.uk.

If you want to apply to a Rent Assessment Committee you should consult an experienced adviser, for example, a Citizens Advice Bureau. If you need help paying the rent you may be able to claim housing benefit. You may also be entitled to other benefits if you are on a low income or you are unemployed.

To work out which other benefits you may be entitled to, you should consult an experienced adviser, for example, a Citizens Advice Bureau.

Affordable rent

Affordable rent is a type of social housing provided in England by social housing landlords.

The rent is called 'affordable' but it is a higher rent than would normally be charged for social housing. The landlord can charge up to 80% of what it would cost if you were renting the property privately. The extra money from affordable rent homes goes towards building more new social housing.

In most cases, tenancies on affordable rent terms are granted by housing associations. Where the landlord is a housing association, the type of tenancy granted is either an assured or an assured shorthold tenancy. In some cases, a local authority may grant a tenancy on affordable rent terms. Where it does, the tenancy type is either a secure or a flexible tenancy.

An affordable rent can be increased once a year. The maximum amount that an affordable rent can be increased by is Retail Price Index (RPI) + 0.5 %.

If you are on benefits or have a low income you may qualify for housing benefit to help pay some or all of the affordable rent.

Repairs and improvements

As a tenant you have the right to have your accommodation kept in a reasonable state of repair. You have also an obligation to look after the accommodation. The tenancy agreement may give more details of both your landlord's and your responsibilities in carrying out repairs and you should check this. We have discussed repairs earlier in the book.

Certain repairs will almost always be your landlord's responsibility, whether or not they are specifically mentioned in the tenancy agreement. These are:-

- the structure and exterior of the premises (such as walls, floors and window frames), and the drains, gutters and external pipes. If the property is a house, the essential means of access to it, such as steps from the street, are also included in 'structure and exterior'. It also includes garden paths and steps
- the water and gas pipes and electrical wiring (including, for example, taps and sockets)
- the basins, sinks, baths and toilets
- fixed heaters (for example, gas fires) and water heaters but not gas or electric cookers.

The Right to repair

Tenants of local authorities and other social landlords (including housing associations) can use 'right to repair' schemes to claim compensation for repairs which the landlord does not carry out within a set timescale.

Local authority tenants have a right to repair scheme which they must follow. Under the scheme, if repairs are not carried out within a fixed time scale, you can notify your landlord that you want a different contractor to do the job. The local authority must appoint a new contractor and set another time limit. You can then claim compensation if the repair is not carried out within the new time limit.

As a local authority tenant, you can currently use the 'right to repair' scheme for repairs which your landlord estimates would cost up to £250. You can also claim up to £50 compensation. Twenty types of repairs qualify for the scheme, including insecure doors, broken entry phone systems, blocked sinks and leaking roofs.

A repair will not qualify for the scheme if the local authority has fewer than 100 properties, is not responsible for the repair or if the authority decides it would cost more than £250.

If you're the tenant of another social landlord, such as a housing association, you are entitled to compensation if you report a repair or maintenance problem which affects your health, safety or security and your landlord fails twice to make the repair within the set timescale.

There is a flat rate award which is currently £10, plus £2 a day up to a total of £50, for each day the repair remains outstanding. A maximum cost for an eligible repair may be set by the individual landlord.

Improvements

As a local authority tenant if you make certain improvements to your home, for example, loft insulation, draught proofing, new baths, basins and toilets and security measures, you can apply for compensation for doing so when you move out. You will not be eligible for this compensation if you buy your home.

Disabled tenants

If you are disabled, you may be able to have alterations carried out to your home. You may first have to get the need for any alterations assessed by the social services department. Alterations could include the installation of a stair lift or hoist or adaptation of a bathroom or toilet.

If you want to get an alteration carried out you should consult an experienced adviser, for example, at a Citizens Advice Bureau.

A disabled tenant may also be able to get a disabled facilities grant to make the home more suitable.

Gas appliances

Your landlord must make sure that any gas appliances in residential premises are safe. They must arrange for safety checks on appliances and fittings to be carried out at least once every twelve months. The inspection must be carried out by someone who is registered with Gas Safety Register. Their website is: www.gassaferegister.co.uk. The landlord must also keep a record of the date of the check, any problems identified and any action taken. As the tenant, you have the right to see this record as long as you give reasonable notice.

If your landlord does not arrange for checks or refuses to allow you to see the record of the check, you could contact the local Health and Safety Executive office.

The right to stay in the accommodation

This is an outline of the rights you have as a tenant of a local authority, housing association or housing co-operative to stay in your accommodation and how you can be evicted.

Secure tenants

As a secure tenant you have the right to stay in the accommodation as long as you keep to the terms of the tenancy agreement with your landlord. However, if the tenancy agreement is broken, for example, because of rent arrears or nuisance to neighbours, your landlord can serve a notice on you and apply to the county court for eviction.

A social housing landlord can only evict you if they give you the proper notice and if one of the 'grounds for possession' applies.

What constitutes 'grounds for possession' is complicated and someone whose landlord is seeking eviction should consult an experienced adviser, for example, at a Citizens Advice Bureau.

. The landlord must apply to the county court to seek possession of the property and a secure tenant can only be evicted if the court grants a possession order to the landlord.

Assured tenants

As an assured tenant you have the right to stay in the accommodation as long as you keep to the terms of the tenancy agreement with your landlord. However, if the tenancy agreement is broken, for example, because of rent arrears or nuisance to neighbours, your landlord can serve a notice on you.

The housing association will then have to obtain a possession order from the county court by proving that one of the 'grounds for possession' applies. We discussed grounds for possession earlier in the book.

Social housing tenancies and discrimination

When renting accommodation from a local authority, housing association or other social landlord, they must not discriminate against you because of your disability, gender reassignment, pregnancy and maternity, race, religion or belief, sex or sexual orientation.

This means that they are not allowed to:

- rent a property to you on worse terms than other tenants
- treat you differently from other tenants in the way you are allowed to use facilities such as a laundry or a garden
- evict or harass you because of discrimination
- charge you higher rent than other tenants
- refuse to re-house you because of discrimination
- refuse to carry out repairs to your home because of disrimination
- refuse to make reasonable changes to a property or a term in the tenancy agreement which would allow a disabled person to live there.

If you think your landlord is discriminating against you, you should get advice from an experienced adviser, for example, at a Citizens Advice Bureau.

Introductory tenants

Some local authorities make all new tenants introductory tenants for the first 12 months of the tenancy.

Rights of introductory tenants

Introductory tenants have some but not all of the rights of secure tenants. The table overleaf shows your rights as an introductory tenant compared with secure tenants.

Statutory right	Secure tenant	Introductory tenant
Right to succession by partners or in some cases family members	yes	yes
Right to repair	yes	yes
Right to assign	yes	no
Right to buy	yes	no, but period spent as an introductory tenant counts towards the discount
Right to take in lodgers	yes	no
Right to sub-let part of your home	yes	no
Right to do improvements	yes	no
Right to exchange your home with certain other tenants	yes	no
Right to vote prior to transfer to new landlord	yes	no
Right to be consulted on housing management issues	yes	yes
Right to be consulted on decision to delegate housing management	yes	yes
Right to participate in housing management contract monitoring	yes	yes

Ending an introductory tenancy

At the end of the twelve months, provided there have been no possession proceedings against you, the introductory tenancy will usually be converted by your landlord to a secure tenancy. However, your landlord may decide to extend the introductory tenancy for a further six months. If this happens, you will be told the reasons for the decision and given the chance to ask for the decision to be reviewed.

Possession proceedings

It is very easy for a landlord to evict an introductory tenant. If you have received a notice from the landlord stating that they intend to evict you and take possession of the property, you should immediately consult an experienced adviser, for example, at a Citizens Advice Bureau.

Flexible tenants

Flexible tenancies are a type of tenancy that can be granted by local authority landlords in England, from 1 April 2012. Not all local authorities offer them.

A flexible tenancy is similar to a local authority secure tenancy. However, a secure tenancy is periodic, which means that it lasts for an indefinite period of time. Periodic tenancies are often called 'lifetime tenancies'. In contrast, a flexible tenancy lasts for a fixed period of time. In most cases, a flexible tenancy will last for at least five years.

A local authority has to serve a written notice on you before a flexible tenancy can start. The notice must tell you that the tenancy you're being offered is a flexible tenancy, and what the terms of the tenancy are.

Flexible tenants have a number of legal rights, many of which are similar to the rights of secure tenants. For example, the right to pass on your tenancy when you're alive or when you die, the right to exchange your home with certain other tenants, and the right to buy your home.

A local authority doesn't have to grant you another tenancy when the fixed term of the flexible tenancy comes to an end. You can ask the local authority to review its decision not to grant you another tenancy. The review will consider if your landlord has followed its policies and procedures when making that decision.

If you are not given another tenancy when your flexible tenancy comes to an end, the local authority will take action to evict you.

Right-to-buy.

Perhaps the most valuable right enjoyed by a secure tenant is the right to buy either the freehold, in the case of a house, or the leasehold, in the case of a flat. In order to claim this right there is also a residence qualification to fulfill. The tenant, or the tenants spouse must have been resident as a secure tenant (not necessarily in the same property) for five years prior to the application to buy. Currently, the government is in the process of extending the right to buy to Housing Association tenants and reducing the residence requirements.

Discounts

If you qualify for Right to Buy, you can get a discount on the market value of your home when you buy it.

The maximum discount is £80,900 (2018) across England, except in London boroughs where it's £108,000. The discount is based on:

- how long you've been a tenant with a public sector landlord
- the type of property you're buying (a flat or a house)
- the value of your home

If you're buying with someone else, you count the years of whoever's been a public sector tenant the longest.

You'll usually have to repay some or all your discount if you sell your home within 5 years.

The discount you get might be reduced if you've used Right to Buy in the past.

Working out the discount

There are different discount levels for houses and flats.

For houses you get a 35% discount if you've been a public sector tenant for between 3 and 5 years. For every extra year you've been a public sector tenant, the discount goes up by 1%, up to a maximum of 70% – or £80,900 across England and £108,000 in London boroughs (whichever is lower).

For flats you get a 50% discount if you've been a public sector tenant for between 3 and 5 years. For every extra year you've been a public sector tenant, the discount goes up by 2%, up to a maximum of 70% – or

£80,900 across England and £108,000 in London boroughs (whichever is lower).

If your landlord has spent money on your home
Your discount will be less if your landlord has spent money building or maintaining your home:

- in the last 10 years - if your landlord built or acquired your home before 2 April 2012
- in the last 15 years - if you are buying your home through Preserved Right to Buy, or if your landlord acquired your home after 2 April 2012

If your landlord has spent more money than your home is now worth, you won't get any discount.

Social HomeBuy
If you can't afford to buy your home through Right to Buy, you may still be able to buy a share of it through social homebuy. With Social HomeBuy, you buy a share of your council or housing association home and pay rent on the rest of it.

Discounts
You'll get a discount of between £9,000 and £16,000 on the value of your home, depending on:

- where your home is
- the size of the share you're buying

If you want to buy another share in your home later on, you'll get a discount on that too.
Buying more of your home later
You must buy at least 25% of your home. You can buy more later, until you own 100%. This is called 'staircasing'.

If you buy more of your home, your rent will go down - because it's based on how much of the property you rent. Your landlord can charge rent of up to 3% of the value of their share of your home, per year.

Example

Your home is worth £240,000 and you buy a 50% share. Your landlord charges you 3% rent on their 50% share. 3% of £120,000 is £3,600 per year. This works out at £300 per month for you to pay in rent.

Who can't apply

You can't use Social HomeBuy if:

- you have an assured shorthold tenancy
- you're being made bankrupt
- a court has ordered you to leave your home
- your landlord is taking action against you for rent arrears, anti-social behaviour or for breaking your tenancy agreement

Not all local councils or housing associations have joined the scheme. Check with your landlord to find out if they belong to the scheme and whether your home is included.

Right to acquire

Right to Acquire allows most housing association tenants to buy their home at a discount. You apply using the Right to Acquire application form.

You can apply to buy your housing association home if you've had a public sector landlord for 3 years. These landlords include:

- housing associations
- councils
- the armed services
- NHS trusts and foundation trusts

Eligible properties

Your property must either have been:

- built or bought by a housing association after 31 March 1997 (and funded through a social housing grant provided by the Housing Corporation or local council)
- transferred from a local council to a housing association after 31 March 1997
- Your landlord must be registered with the Homes and Communities Agency.

The home you want to buy must also be:

- a self-contained property
- your only or main home

Who doesn't qualify

You can't use Right to Acquire if:

- you're being made bankrupt
- a court has ordered you to leave your home
- you're a council tenant – you may be able to use Right to Buy instead
- you have 'Preserved Right to Buy'

Discounts

You can get a discount of between £9,000 and £16,000 on the price of your property. The amount of discount you'll get depends on where you live in the

Succession and assured and secure tenancies

For secure tenancies, it can be found under Section 160 of the Localism Act 2011; while for assured tenancies, it is under Section 161 of the same Act.

It remains that there can only be one succession, and that when one joint tenant dies this counts as one succession.

Before the Localism Act, a wide range of family members were able to succeed to a tenancy on the death of a secure tenant, including: civil partners, parents, grandparents, children, grandchildren, aunts, uncles, nieces, nephews, and adopted children. A full list is set out at Section 113 of the Housing Act 1985.

Civil partners and spouses are entitled to succeed so long as they were occupying the property as their only or principal home at the date of the death.

Other family members were required to prove they had occupied the property as their only or principal home for 12 months prior to the death of the tenant whose tenancy they wish to succeed.

Under the provisions of Section 17 Housing Act 1988, a spouse, civil partner or someone living with the tenant as a spouse or civil partner is entitled to succeed to the tenancy provided they occupied the property as their only or principal home at the date of death.

It was very common to see landlords of assured tenants including wider succession rights in their tenancy agreements, thus allowing the tenant to benefit from a wider list of family members who would be entitled to succeed to the tenancy provided they had occupied the property as their only or principal home as the death of the tenant.

Automatic right to succession
Section 160 of the Localism Act 2011 provides that secure tenancies which started after 1 April 2012 are limited to the succession of spouses or civil partners. This is an automatic right.

The wider group of family members who have traditionally succeeded to a secure tenancy by virtue of being listed in Section 113 of the Housing Act 1985 do not automatically receive statutory succession. The landlord can make express provision in the tenancy agreement to expand the group of individuals that can succeed.

Section 161 of the Localism Act 2011 provides that assured tenancies which started after 1 April 2012 containing a clause which expands the statutory group of individuals entitled to succeed to include family members; the family member who is entitled to succeed will enjoy a statutory succession. Family members may only succeed if there is express provision in the tenancy agreement.

Unlike before, those listed and who become entitled to succeed under an express term of a tenancy agreement will enjoy a statutory succession, so that no new tenancy is required.

****

7

The 1988 Housing Act, (as amended)-Assured Tenancies

Most people, when renting a property through the private sector will become assured tenants, or to be exact assured shorthold tenants, which is a derivation of an assured tenancy. In this chapter we will elaborate on the exact nature of these tenancies.

The assured tenant

As we have seen, with the exception of local authority secure tenancies, and also various other types of agreements, such as company lets, all tenancies, are known as assured tenancies. An assured shorthold, which is the most common form of tenancy used by the private landlord nowadays, is one type of assured tenancy, and is for a fixed term of six months minimum and can be brought to an end with two months notice by serving a section 21 (of the Housing Act 1988) notice (see below) .

It is important to note that all tenancies signed after February 1997 are assured shorthold agreements unless otherwise stated.

Assured tenancies are governed by the 1988 Housing Act, as amended by the 1996 Housing Act. It is to these Acts, or outlines of the Acts that the tenant must refer when intending to sign a tenancy for a residential property.

For a tenancy to be assured, three conditions must be fulfilled:

1. The premises must be a dwelling house. This basically means any premises which can be lived in. Business premises will normally fall outside this interpretation.
2. There must exist a particular relationship between landlord and tenant.

In other words there must exist a tenancy agreement. For example, a license to occupy, as in the case of students, or accommodation occupied as a result of work, cannot be seen as a tenancy. Following on from this, the accommodation must be let as a single unit. The tenant, who must be an individual, must normally be able to sleep, cook and eat in the accommodation. Sharing of bathroom facilities will not prevent a tenancy being an assured tenancy but shared cooking or other facilities, such as a living room, will.

3. The third requirement for an assured tenancy is that the tenant must occupy the dwelling as his or her only or principal home. In situations involving joint tenants at least one of them must occupy.

Tenancies that are not assured

A tenancy agreement will not be assured if one of the following conditions applies:

-The tenancy or the contract was entered into before 15th January 1989;

-If no rent is payable or if only a low rent amounting to less than two thirds of the present ratable value of the property is payable;

-If the premises are let for business purposes or for mixed residential and business purposes;

-If part of the dwelling house is licensed for the sale of liquor for consumption on the premises. This does not include the publican who lets out a flat;

-If the dwelling house is let with more than two acres of agricultural land;

-If the dwelling house is part of an agricultural holding and is occupied in relation to carrying out work on the holding;

-If the premises are let by a specified institution to students, i.e., halls of residence;

-If the premises are let for the purpose of a holiday;

-Where there is a resident landlord, e.g., in the case where the landlord has let one of his rooms but continues to live in the house;

-If the landlord is the Crown (the monarchy) or a government department. Certain lettings by the Crown are capable of being assured, such as some lettings by the Crown Estate Commissioners;

-If the landlord is a local authority, a fully mutual housing association (this is where you have to be a shareholder to be a tenant) a newly created Housing Action Trust or any similar body listed in the 1988 Housing Act.

-If the letting is transitional such as a tenancy continuing in its original form until phased out, such as:

-A protected tenancy under the 1977 Rent Act;

-Secure tenancy granted before 1st January 1989, e.g., from a local authority or housing association. These tenancies are governed by the 1985 Housing Act).

The Assured Shorthold tenancy

The assured shorthold tenancy as we have seen, is the most common form of tenancy used in the private sector. The main principle of the assured shorthold tenancy is that it is issued for a period of six months minimum and can be brought to an end by the landlord serving two-months notice on the tenant (Section 21 notice).

New rules for Section 21 notices

If the tenancy started or was renewed on or after 1 October 2015 a landlord will need to use the new prescribed Section 21 notice form (6a).

Section 21 pre-requisites

A landlord cannot serve a valid section 21 notice if:

- They have taken a deposit and not protected and/or served the prescribed information and/or

- They have failed to obtained a license for an HMO property which requires one

If the tenancy was in England and started or was renewed on or after 1 October 2015 a landlord must also have served on their tenant (and you should get proof of service for all these:

- an EPC
- a Gas Safety Certificate, and
- the latest version of the Government's "How to Rent" Guide.

Plus a landlord cannot serve a section 21 notice if their Local Authority has served one of 3 specified notices (the most important being an improvement notice) on them within the past six months in respect of the poor condition of the rental property.

Also, if the tenant complained about the issues covered by the notice prior to this – any Section 21 notice served since the complaint and before the Local Authority notice was served will also be invalid.

The notice period must not be less than two months and must not end before the end of the fixed term (if this has not ended at the time the landlord served their notice)

If this is a periodic tenancy where the period (rent payment period) is more than monthly (e.g., a quarterly or six month periodic tenancy), then the notice period must be at least one full tenancy period.

The notice period does not have to end on a particular day in the month, as was required under the old rules – the landlord just needs to make sure that the notice period is sufficient – minimum of 2 months.

Conditions for an assured shorthold tenancy

Any property let on an assured tenancy can be let on an assured shorthold, providing the following three conditions are met:

- The tenancy must be for a fixed term of not less than six months.
- The agreement cannot contain powers which enable the landlord to end the tenancy before six months. This does not include the

right of the landlord to enforce the grounds for possession, which will be approximately the same as those for the assured tenancy

- A notice must be served before any rent increase giving one months clear notice and providing details of the rent increase.

If the landlord wishes to get possession of his/her property, in this case before the expiry of the contractual term, the landlord has to gain a court order. A notice of seeking possession must be served, giving fourteen days notice and following similar grounds of possession as an assured tenancy.

The landlord cannot simply tell a tenant to leave before the end of the agreed term.

If the tenancy runs on after the end of the fixed term then the landlord can regain possession by giving the required two months notice, as mentioned above.

At the end of the term for which the assured shorthold tenancy has been granted, the landlord has an automatic right to possession.

An assured shorthold tenancy will become periodic (will run from week to week) when the initial term of six months has elapsed and the landlord has not brought the tenancy to an end. A periodic tenancy is brought to an end with two months notice. Assured shorthold tenants can be evicted only on certain grounds, some discretionary, some mandatory (see below).

In order for the landlord of an assured shorthold tenant to regain possession of the property, a notice of seeking possession (of property) must be served, giving fourteen days notice of expiry and stating the ground for possession. A copy of this notice is shown in Appendix 2. This notice is similar to a notice to quit, discussed in the previous chapter. Following the fourteen days a court order must be obtained. Although gaining a court order is not complicated, a solicitor will usually be used. Court costs can be awarded against the tenant.

Security of tenure: The ways in which a tenant can lose their home as an assured shorthold tenant

There are a number of circumstances called grounds (mandatory and discretionary) whereby a landlord can start a court action to evict a tenant. The following are the *mandatory* grounds (where the judge must give the landlord possession) and *discretionary* grounds (where the judge does not have to give the landlord possession) on which a court can order possession if the home is subject to an assured tenancy.

The mandatory grounds for possession of a property let on an assured (shorthold) tenancy

There are eight mandatory grounds for possession, which, if proved, leave the court with no choice but to make an order for possession. It is very important that you understand these.

Ground One is used where the landlord has served a notice, no later than at the beginning of the tenancy, warning the tenant that this ground may be used against him/her. This ground is used where the landlord wishes to recover the property as his or her principal (first and only) home or the spouse's (wife's or husbands) principal home. *The ground is not available to a person who bought the premises for gain (profit) whilst they were occupied.*

Ground Two is available where the property is subject to a mortgage and if the landlord does not pay the mortgage, could lose the home.

Grounds Three and Four relate to holiday lettings.

Ground Five is a special one, applicable to ministers of religion.

Ground Six relates to the demolition or reconstruction of the property.

Ground Seven applies if a tenant dies and in his will leaves the tenancy to someone else: but the landlord must start proceedings against the new tenant within a year of the death if he wants to evict the new tenant.

Ground Eight concerns rent arrears. This ground applies if, both at the date of the serving of the notice seeking possession and at the date of the hearing of the action, the rent is at least 8 weeks in arrears or two months in arrears. This is the main ground used by landlords when rent is not being paid.

The discretionary grounds for possession of a property, which is let on an assured tenancy

As we have seen, the discretionary grounds for possession are those in relation to which the court has some powers over whether or not the landlord can evict. In other words, the final decision is left to the judge. Often the judge will prefer to grant a suspended order first, unless the circumstances are dramatic.

Ground Nine applies when suitable alternative accommodation is available or will be when the possession order takes effect. As we have seen, if the landlord wishes to obtain possession of his or her property in order to use it for other purposes then suitable alternative accommodation has to be provided.

Ground Ten deals with rent arrears as does *ground eleven*. These grounds are distinct from the mandatory grounds, as there does not have to be a fixed arrear in terms of time scale, e.g., 8 weeks. The judge, therefore, has some choice as to whether or not to evict. In practice, this ground will not be relevant to managers of assured shorthold tenancies.

Ground Twelve concerns any broken obligation of the tenancy. As we have seen with the protected tenancy, there are a number of conditions of the tenancy agreement, such as the requirement not to racially or sexually harass a neighbor. Ground Twelve will be used if these conditions are broken.

Ground Thirteen deals with the deterioration of the dwelling as a result of a tenant's neglect. This is connected with the structure of the property and is the same as for a protected tenancy. It puts the responsibility on the tenant to look after the premises.

Ground Fourteen concerns nuisance, annoyance and illegal or immoral use. This is where a tenant or anyone connected with the tenant has caused a nuisance to neighbors.

Ground 14A this ground deals with domestic violence.

Ground 15 concerns the condition of the furniture and tenants neglect. As Ground thirteen puts some responsibility on the tenant to look after the structure of the building so Ground Fifteen makes the tenant responsible for the furniture and fittings.

Ground 16 covers former employees. The premises were let to a former tenant by a landlord seeking possession and the tenant has ceased to be in that employment.

Ground 17 is where a person or that persons agents makes a false or reckless statement and this has caused the landlord to grant the tenancy under false pretences.

The description of the grounds above is intended as a guide only. A fuller description is contained within the 1988 Housing Act, section 7, Schedule two,) as amended by the 1996 Housing Act) which is available at reference libraries.

Fast track possession

In November 1993, following changes to the County Court Rules, a facility was introduced which enabled landlords of tenants with assured shorthold tenancies to apply for possession of their property without the usual time delay involved in waiting for a court date and attendance at court.

This is known as "fast track possession" It cannot be used for rent arrears or other grounds. It is used to gain possession of a property when the fixed term of six months or more has come to an end and the tenant will not move.

Payment of rent

If the landlord wishes to raise rent, at least one month's minimum notice must be given. The rent cannot be raised more than once for the same tenant in one year. Tenants have the right to challenge a rent increase if they think it is unfair by referring the rent to a Rent Assessment Committee. The committee will prevent the landlord from raising the rent above the ordinary market rent for that type of property. We will be discussing rent and rent control further on in this book.

****

8

Joint Tenancies

Although it is the normal state of affairs for a tenancy agreement to be granted to one person, this is not always the case.

A tenancy can also be granted to two or more people and is then known as a *joint tenancy*. The position of joint tenants is exactly the same as that of single tenants. In other words, there is still one tenancy even though it is shared. Each tenant is responsible for paying the rent and observing the terms and conditions of the tenancy agreement. No one joint tenant can prevent another joint tenant's access to the premises. If one of the joint tenants dies then his or her interest will automatically pass to the remaining joint tenants. A joint tenant cannot dispose of his or her interest in a will.

Joint tenants usually all have the same rights and responsibilities in their rented home and are all responsible for paying the rent.

Joint Tenancy agreements

A person has a joint tenancy if they and their flatmates or housemates all signed a single tenancy agreement with a landlord when they moved in. This means that they all have the same rights and responsibilities. If each of them signed a separate agreement with the landlord, you have separate tenancies.

Rent liability when a joint tenant

Joint tenants are all jointly and individually responsible for paying the rent. This means that if one of them moves out without giving notice or is not paying their share, the other joint tenants are responsible for paying it for them. If none of them pay your rent, their landlord can ask any one of them to pay the full amount. All the joint tenants are usually also responsible for paying gas and electricity bills.

Tenancy deposits

When a person moves into private rented accommodation, they usually need to pay a deposit to cover any damage or unpaid rent. the deposit has to be put into a tenancy deposit scheme.

Deductions from a tenancy deposit

The landlord normally takes a single deposit for the whole of the tenancy. If one joint tenant fails to pay their share of the rent or if they cause damage to the property, the landlord is entitled to deduct the shortfall or damage from the deposit. All joint tenants decide how to divide up the remaining deposit when it is returned.

Tenancy deposits when a joint tenant moves out

If tenants are replacing another tenant who is moving out, they may ask them to pay the deposit to them instead. This may not be a good idea. If the tenant who is moving out has caused any damage to the property or left any unpaid bills, the landlord can deduct these costs from the deposit when they move out, which could leave you out of pocket.

Permission for changes

Permission is needed from the other joint tenants if a tenant wants to carry out improvements to the property or pass on or assign their tenancy to someone else. In most cases they also need their landlord's permission to do any of these things, or if they want to take in a lodger.

Ending a joint tenancy: when one person leaves

The rules on how and when a tenancy can be ended depend on whether the tenancy is fixed-term (for a set period of time) or periodic (rolling from week to week or month to month). If a tenant wants to leave, they should discuss this with the other joint tenants before they take any action.

A fixed-term tenancy cannot be ended early unless all of the joint tenants agree and either:

- the landlord agrees that the tenancy can end early (this is called a 'surrender'), or

- there is a 'break clause' in the tenancy agreement, which allows them to give notice and leave early

If a tenant has a periodic tenancy, or the fixed-term has ended and the tenancy has not been renewed, one tenant can end the whole tenancy and does not need the agreement of the other joint tenants. The landlord must be given a valid written notice and there are special rules about how and when this must be done.

Leaving a joint tenancy

If a tenant wants to leave a joint tenancy, it is usually best to discuss it with the other joint tenants before taking any action. If the other joint tenant(s) don't want to move out, they can try to negotiate a new agreement with the landlord. The remaining tenants may be able to find another person to take on the tenancy of the person who wants to leave (the landlord would have to agree to this), or agree with the other joint tenants to stay on and pay the extra rent themselves. The landlord may decide to: give the other tenants a new tenancy agreement, listing the new tenants (in practice, your landlord might not bother to do this)

- accept the rent from the new tenant — in which case the new tenant should have the same rights as a tenant whose name is actually on the tenancy agreement

Eviction of joint tenants

A landlord cannot evict one joint tenant without evicting all the others. Instead, the landlord may be able to end the tenancy (using the procedures for eviction) and offer a new one to the remaining tenants.

Relationship breakdown

In the event of a relationship breakdown a tenant may have rights that you are not aware of.

For example:

- it may be possible for the joint tenancy to be transferred into one person's name – this can sometimes be done even if the other joint tenant won't agree to it
- it may be possible to stop the other joint tenant from ending the tenancy by applying for an occupation order or an injunction

If a tenant has experienced domestic violence, it may be possible to keep the perpetrator out of the home or to take legal action such as an injunction.

****

9

Private Tenancies in Scotland

The law governing the relationship between private landlords and tenants in Scotland is different to that in England. Since the beginning of 1989, new private sector tenancies in Scotland were covered by the Housing (Scotland) Act 1988. Following the passage of this Act, private sector tenants no longer had any protection as far as rent levels were concerned and tenants enjoyed less security of tenure. However, **The Private Housing (Tenancies) (Scotland) Act 2016**, passed by the Scottish Parliament and coming into force on 1st December 2017 has changed the law concerning private tenancies in Scotland. The main provisions of the Act are outlined below.

The new Private Residential Tenancy

On 1 December 2017 a new type of tenancy came into force, called the private residential tenancy, it replaced assured and short assured tenancy agreements for all new tenancies from 1st December 2017. as a result of passing of The Private Housing (Tenancies) (Scotland) Act 2016. The new Scottish Private Residential Tenancy, (SPRT) will deliver improved security of tenure for tenants, including students in smaller purpose built and mainstream private rented accommodation, and also the power for local authorities to designate rent pressure zones within their jurisdiction. There will also be streamlined procedures for starting and ending a tenancy and a model agreement for landlords and tenants.

The SPRT will become the standard tenancy agreement between residential landlords and tenants and will replace the most common types of residential tenancies in Scotland – the Short Assured Tenancy and the Assured Tenancy.

What changes has the private residential tenancy brought in?

Any tenancy that started on or after 1 December 2017 will be a private residential tenancy. These new tenancies will bring in changes and improvements to the private rented sector, including:

- **No more fixed terms** - private residential tenancies are open ended, meaning a landlord can't ask a tenant to leave just because they have been in the property for 6 months as they can with a short assured tenancy.
- **Rent increases** – a tenant's rent can only be increased once every 12 months (with 3 months notice) and if they think the proposed increase is unfair they can refer it to a rent officer.
- **Longer notice period** - if a tenant has lived in a property for longer than 6 months the landlord will have to give them at least 84 days notice to leave (unless they have broken a term in the tenancy).
- **Simpler notices** - the notice to quit process has been scrapped and replaced by a simpler notice to leave process.
- **Model tenancy agreement** - the Scottish Government have published a model private residential tenancy that can be used by landlords to set up a tenancy.

Person already an assured/short assured tenant

If a tenant was already renting and were an assured or short assured tenant, on 1 December 2017, their tenancy will continue as normal until they or their landlord brings it to an end following the correct procedure. If a landlord then offers a tenant a new tenancy this will be a private residential tenancy.

What is a private residential tenancy?

A private residential tenancy is one that meets the following conditions:

- the tenancy started on or after 1 December 2017
- it is let to a person as a separate dwelling (home)

- the person must be an individual, meaning not a company
- it's their main or only home
- they must have a lease (although a written agreement not needed for a lease to exist)
- the tenancy is not a exemptions tenancy, as listed below.

Tenancy agreements

A person have the right to a tenancy agreement, which can be either a written or electronic copy, within 28 days of the start of the tenancy.

The Scottish Government has published a model tenancy that a landlord can use to set up a tenancy. This tenancy plus a set of notes that a landlord must give to the tenant can be accessed at www.mygov.scot/tenancy-agreement-scotland. This tenancy agreement contains certain statutory terms that outline both parties rights and obligations including:

- The tenant's and landlord/letting agent's contact details
- The address and details of the rented property
- The start date of the tenancy
- How much the rent is and how it can be increased
- How much the deposit is and information about how it will be registered
- Who is responsible for insuring the property.
- The tenant has to inform the landlord when they are going to be absent from the property for more than 14 days
- The tenant will take reasonable care of the property
- The condition that the landlord must make sure the property is in, including the repairing standard.
- That the tenant must inform the landlord the need of any repairs.
- That the tenant will give reasonable access to the property, when the landlord has given at least 48 hours notice
- The process that the tenancy can be brought to an end

If a landlord uses the Scottish Government's' model tenancy they should also give the tenant the 'Easy Read Notes' which will explain the tenancy terms in plain English. If a landlord does not use the model tenancy they must give the tenant the private residential tenancy statutory terms: supporting notes, with their lease, which will explains the basic set of terms that a landlord has to include in the lease.

Rent Increases

The rent can only be increased once every 12 months and the landlord needs to give a tenant 3 months notice, using the correct notice of the rent increase. If the tenant doesn't agree to the rent increase they can refer it to the local rent officer. The referral to the rent officer must be done within 21 days of receiving the rent increase notice.

When a referral made to the rent officer, they will first issue a provisional order which will suggest the amount the rent can be increased. The tenant will have 14 days from the date the provisional order is issued to request a reconsideration. If the tenant requests a reconsideration the rent officer will look at it again before making a final order and telling them the date that the increase will take place.

Ending a tenancy

If a tenant wants to end the tenancy, then they will have to give the landlord 28 days notice in writing. The notice has to state the day on which the tenancy is to end, normally the day after notice period has expired.

The tenant can agree a different notice period with the landlord as long it is in writing. If there is no agreed notice then 28 days notice is the minimum required.

Landlord access

The tenant has to allow reasonable access to the landlord to carry out repairs, inspections, or valuations when:

- the landlord has given at least 48 hours' written notice, or

- access is required urgently for the landlord to view or carry out works in relation to the repairing standard

If a tenant refuses access the landlord can make an application to the First Tier Tribunal Housing and Property Chamber who may make an order allowing them access.

Getting repairs carried out

As with other tenancies, the landlord has to keep the property wind and watertight, and in a condition that is safe to live in. The landlord is also responsible for making sure that the property repairing standard is met. This is a basic level of repair that is required by law. The landlord must give the tenant information on the repairing standard and what they can do if the property does not meet it.   If a tenant wants to carry out work on their home, such as redecorating or installing a second phone line, they will need to seek permission from the landlord. Some tenancy agreements will include a clause telling the tenant whether they can carry out this kind of work.

Can a tenant sublet or pass their tenancy on to someone else?

A tenant cannot sublet, take in a lodger or pass their tenancy on to someone else before first getting written agreement from the landlord.

Tenancies that cannot be private residential tenancy

Almost all new private tenancies created on or after 1st December 2017 will be private residential tenancies. However, there are a number of exemptions, including the following:

- Tenancies at a low rent
- Tenancies of shops
- Licensed premises
- Tenancies of agricultural land
- Lettings to students (meaning purpose built student accommodation)
- Holiday lettings

- Resident landlords
- Police Housing
- Military Housing
- Social Housing
- Sublet, assigned etc. social housing
- Homeless persons
- Persons on probation or released from prison etc.
- Accommodation for asylum seekers
- Displaced persons
- Shared ownership
- Tenancies under previous legislation
- Assured or short assured tenancies

Short assured and assured tenancies

Most residential lettings in Scotland made after 2 January 1989 and before 1st December 2017 are short assured tenancies. Those that aren't short assured are normally assured tenancies.

Short assured tenancies

This was the most common type of tenancy. A short assured tenancy makes it easier for a landlord to get a property than an assured tenancy. Before any agreement is signed, a landlord must use form AT5 to tell new tenants that the tenancy will be a short assured tenancy. (see appendix). If they don't, the tenancy will automatically be an assured tenancy. Initially, a short assured tenancy must be for 6 months or more. After the first 6 months, the tenancy can be renewed for a shorter period.

Assured tenancies

At the beginning of an assured tenancy, it will be classed as a 'contractual assured tenancy' for a fixed period of time. The tenancy automatically becomes a 'statutory assured tenancy' if:

- the landlord ends the tenancy by issuing a notice to quit (eg because they want to change the agreement) and the tenant stays in the property
- the fixed period covered by the tenancy comes to an end and the tenant stays in the property

There are different rights and responsibilities on both landlord and tenant depending on the type of assured tenancy.

Other types of tenancy

Most tenancies in Scotland issued before December 2017 are short assured or assured tenancies. The other tenancy types are:

- 'common law' tenancy - if a tenant shares their home as a lodger
- regulated tenancy - the most common form of tenancy before 1989
- agricultural tenancy
- crofting tenancy

'Common law' tenancies

If a landlord is sharing their house or flat with their tenants, they can't use the short assured or assured tenancy. Instead, they will automatically have what is known as a 'common law tenancy'. The tenant doesn't have to have a written contract but the landlord may use a lodger agreement to create a contract between them and the tenant - so both are clear about what has been agreed. (see appendix for sample lodger agreement).

Regulated tenancies

Tenancies created before 2 January 1989 are generally regulated tenancies. As not many exist we will not be describing them further here.

Agricultural tenancies

There are 3 types of agricultural tenancy:

- limited duration tenancy - if the lease is for more than 5 years
- short limited duration tenancy - if the lease is for 5 years or less
- 1991 Act tenancy - if the tenancy began before 2003

All agricultural tenants have the right to:

- a written lease
- compensation at the end of the tenancy for any improvements they made to the land during their tenancy
- leave the tenancy to a spouse or relative in their will
- If the lease is over 5 years, agricultural tenants can also:

- pass their tenancy on to a relative or spouse within their lifetime
- use the land for non-agricultural purposes
- Tenants with a 1991 Act tenancy have the right to buy the land they are leasing.

If there's a house on the land, both landlord and tenant have obligations to keep it in good repair.

Crofting tenancies

Crofting is a system of landholding unique to the Highlands and Islands of Scotland. Usually, the crofter holds the croft on the 'statutory conditions' and doesn't have a written lease. Crofting is regulated by the Crofting Commission. The tenant must get written agreement from the Commission if you want to make any changes to a crofting tenancy (including a change of tenant).

What the landlord must include in a tenancy agreement

If a landlord used an assured or short assured tenancy, the agreement must be written down. It must include:

- the names of all people involved
- the rental price and how it's paid

- the deposit amount and how it will be protected (see below)
- when the deposit can be fully or partly withheld (eg to repair damage caused by tenants)
- the property address
- the start and end date of the tenancy
- any tenant or landlord obligations
- who's responsible for minor repairs
- which bills your tenants are responsible for
- a statement telling the tenant that antisocial behaviour is a breach of the agreement

For other types of tenancy, it's still good practice to put the agreement in writing. including other information To avoid any confusion later, the landlord can include other information in the agreement, such as:

- whether the tenancy can be ended early and how this can be done
- information on how and when the rent will be reviewed
- whether the property can be let to someone else (sublet) or have lodgers

Changes to tenancy agreements

The landlord must get the agreement of their tenants if they want to make changes to the terms of their tenancy agreement.

Preventing discrimination

Unless the landlord have a very strong reason, they must change anything in a tenancy agreement that might discriminate against tenants on the grounds of:

- gender
- sexual orientation
- disability (or because of something connected with their disability)
- religion or belief

- being a transsexual person
- the tenant being pregnant or having a baby

Ending a Short assured tenancy

To get a property back, the landlord must give tenants a 'notice to quit' and a 'Section 33 notice'. For a short assured tenancy, the minimum notice period is 40 days if the tenancy is for 6 months or longer.

For a tenancy that is continuing on a month by month basis after the original period has ended, the notice period is a minimum of 28 days. The landlord must give 2 months notice when giving a Section 33 notice. They can issue both the notice to quit and Section 33 notice at the same time. (see appendix)

Other tenancy types (excluding the new private residential tenancy)

For other tenancy types the landlord must give at least:

- 28 days if the tenancy is for up to 1 month
- 31 days if the tenancy is for up to 3 months
- 40 days if the tenancy is for more than 3 months

Ending a tenancy early

A landlord can end a tenancy early if:

- the tenant breaks a condition of the tenancy agreement
- landlord and tenant agree to end the tenancy

If tenants don't leave

If the notice period expires and tenants don't leave the property, the landlord can start the process of eviction through the courts. A landlord must tell tenants of their intention to get a court order by giving them a 'notice of intention to raise proceedings' (AT6) (see appendix).

If tenants want to leave

The tenancy agreement should say how much notice tenants need to give before they can leave the property. If the notice isn't mentioned in the tenancy agreement, the minimum notice a tenant can give is:

- 28 days if their tenancy runs on a month-to-month basis (or if it's for less than a month)
- 40 days if their tenancy is for longer than 3 months

Ending a tenancy early

Unless there's a break clause in the tenancy agreement, a landlord can insist that their tenants pay rent until the end of the tenancy. If tenants leave the property without giving notice, or before the notice has run out, they're still responsible for the property and the rent by law.

Houses in multiple occupation (HMOs)

If a tenant is living in a bedsit, shared flat, lodging, shared house, hostel or bed and breakfast accommodation it's likely that they will be living a house in multiple occupation or 'HMO'. A landlord will have an HMO if:

- tenants live with two or more other people, and
- they don't belong to the same family, and
- they share some facilities, e.g. a bathroom or kitchen, and
- the accommodation is their only or main home (if they are a student, their term-time residence counts as their main home).

If they live with a homeowner their family doesnt count as 'qualifying persons' when deciding whether or not a property is an HMO. So for example, if they share accommodation with the owner and one other unrelated lodger, they won't live in an HMO. If they live with the owner and two other unrelated lodgers, they will live in an HMO. Before the council gives a landlord an HMO licence, it will carry out the following checks:

Is the landlord a fit and proper person to hold a licence?
Before it will grant an HMO licence, the council must check that the owner and anyone who manages the property (for example, a letting agent) don't have any criminal convictions, for example, for fraud or theft.

Is the property managed properly?
The council must check that the landlord respects tenants legal rights. They should be given a written tenancy agreement stating clearly what the landlord's responsibilities are, and what the tenants responsibilities are. This should cover things like rent, repairs and other rules. To manage the property properly, the landlord must:

- keep the property and any furniture and fittings in good repair
- deal with the tenant fairly and legally when it comes to rent and other payments, for example they:
- must go through the correct procedure if they want to increase the rent
- cannot resell the tenant gas or electricity at a profit
- not evict the tenant illegally
- make sure that their tenants don't annoy or upset other people living in the area.

Does the property meet the required standards?
To meet the standards expected of an HMO property:

- the rooms must be a decent size, for example, every bedroom should be able to accommodate a bed, a wardrobe and a chest of drawers.
- there must be enough kitchen and bathroom facilities for the number of people living in the property, with adequate hot and cold water supplies.
- adequate fire safety measures must be installed, for example the landlord must provide smoke alarms and self-closing fire doors and make sure there is an emergency escape route.

- all gas and electrical appliances must be safe.
- heating, lighting and ventilation must all be adequate.
- the property should be secure, with good locks on the doors and windows.
- there must be a phone line installed so that tenants can set up a contract with a phone company to supply the service.

Safeguarding Tenancy Deposits

A tenancy deposit scheme is a scheme provided by an independent third party to protect deposits until they are due to be repaid. Three schemes are now operating:

- Letting Protection Service Scotland
- Safedeposits Scotland
- Mydeposits Scotland

Landlord's legal duties

The legal duties on landlords who receive a tenancy deposit are:

- to pay deposits to an approved tenancy deposit scheme
- to provide the tenant with key information about the tenancy and deposit

Key dates for landlords

The dates by which landlords must pay deposits to an approved scheme and provide information to the tenant vary, depending on when the deposit was received:

1. Deposit received prior to 7 March 2011:

Where the tenancy is renewed by express agreement or tacit relocation on or after 2 October 2012 and before 2 April 2013 (Regulation 47(a)) Within 30 working days of renewal. In any other case by 15 May 2013

2. Deposit received on or after 7 March 2011 and before 2 July 2012

By 13 November 2012

3. Deposit received on or after 2 July 2012 and before 2 October 2012

By 13 November 2012

4. Deposit received on or after 2 October 2012

Within 30 working days of the beginning of the tenancy

Information about the schemes

Further details about the individual schemes are available on the individual scheme web sites below. Email addresses and telephone numbers are also included. All three schemes have a range of information available for both landlords (and their agents) as well as tenants and these include how landlords can join the schemes, how to submit deposits, how to ask for repayment of deposits and how the dispute resolution service will work.

Letting Protection Service Scotland

www.lettingprotectionscotland.com

Address:

The Pavilions

Bridgwater Road

Bristol

BS99 6BN

Email contact: events@lettingprotectionscotland.com

Telephone: 0330 303 0031

SafeDeposits Scotland

www.safedepositsscotland.com

Address:

Lower Ground-250 West George Street

Glasgow

G2 4QY

Email contact: info@safedepositsscotland.com

Telephone: 03333 213 136

Mydeposits Scotland

www.mydepositsscotland.co.uk

Address:

Premiere House

Elstree Way

Borehamwood

Hertfordshire

WD6 1JH

Email contact: info@mydepositsscotland.co.uk

Telephone: 0333 321 9402

****

10

The Law and Mobile (Park) Homes and Residential Houseboats

Introduction to park homes

Park Home is the commonly used term for a mobile home (caravan) on a protected site within the meaning of the Mobile Homes Act 1983 (the 1983 Act). A protected site is one that is required to be licensed by a local authority under Part 1 of the Caravan Sites and Control of Development Act 1960 which covers most sites containing wholly residential park homes or a mixture of residential and holiday homes.

If someone has an agreement to live in a 'park home' as their only or main residence on a protected site then they will have the benefit of the rights and protections provided by the 1983 Act which implies a number of important terms into their agreement. These cover such matters as to how the agreement can be terminated, how the annual 'pitch fee' can be changed and the process that needs to be followed when buying or selling (or gifting) the home.

Changes to implied rights under the 1983 Act came into effect on 26 May 2013. These concern the buying, selling or gifting of a park home and the pitch fee review process. Further changes to the licensing of park homes came into effect on 1 April 2014, giving local authorities greater powers to enforce compliance with site licence conditions.

The right to a written agreement and a statement of rights

The site owner must give a person a statement of their legal rights and the terms of their agreement. The agreement cannot change their rights under the Mobile Homes Act. They or the site owner can apply to change the terms of the agreement within six months of the issue of the original agreement. Either side can apply to the county court or an arbitrator, if they cannot agree the terms.

Buying a park home from the site owner

The changes made by the Mobile Homes Act 2013 will have little impact upon the process of purchasing a park home from the site owner. Where buying a park home directly from the site owner (or bringing their own home onto the site) a person can seek to negotiate the terms of their agreement with the site owner, although certain terms will be implied into the agreement by the 1983 Act.

The site owner should provide a person with a written statement setting out the specific terms of their agreement to live in their park home on the site. This must be given to them 28 days before they sign the agreement (or if there is no such agreement at least 28 days before occupation). The terms of the written statement will apply whether or not they are part of any written agreement with the site owner.

The form of the written statement has been prescribed by regulations. The latest version is contained in the Mobile Homes (Written Statement) (England) Regulations 2011 which applies to written statements provided after 30 April 2011.

The written statement contains information about a purchaser's rights and the particulars of the agreement such as the details of the pitch on which the park home rests, the pitch fee, The terms that are implied into the agreement under the 1983 Act including repairing responsibilities and any additional express terms that it is proposed should be included in the agreement.

If a person does not receive a written statement then any express terms in the agreement such as those providing for the payment of the pitch fee cannot be enforced by the site owner.

A person can apply to a tribunal for an order that the written statement is provided by the site owner. The form that should be used is Form PH1.

Other rules

There will often be specific rules that will apply to a particular site (site rules) which deal with such matters as any age restrictions, the use of car parking areas and keeping pets.

Changing the terms of the agreement

The purchaser or the site owner can apply to a tribunal to delete, vary or add an express term within the first six months of the original agreement being made. The form that should be used is Form PH2.

Buying a park home from an existing home owner

Significant changes have been made by the Mobile Homes Act 2013 to the process by which a mobile home is bought and sold in England following changes made by the Mobile Homes Act 2013. These changes mean that as from 26 May 2013 a buyer does not have to have any contact with the site owner before buying the home.

It should be noted that until changes are made to the law that applies in Wales, the consent of the site owner will still be required to purchase a park home there.

What will be the terms of the agreement with the site owner?

The purchaser will be taking over an existing agreement with the site owner and so this will depend upon the particular agreement that was previously made with the site owner for the home to be stationed on the site.

The new process for buying a park home in England

New terms concerning the sale of the park home are now being implied into agreements between park home owners and site owners. These new implied terms vary depending on whether the home was acquired by the current owner on or before 26 May 2013.

However the changes that have been introduced will mean that in all cases the site owner will have no direct involvement in the sale or gift of a park home and any inconsistent provision in the agreement or site rules will not be enforceable.

The process

Once a person has agreed with the seller to purchase the park home, the seller will be required to serve them with a prescribed notice called a Buyer's Information Form at least 28 days before the sale date. This notice will include prescribed information including the proposed sale price and details about the pitch fee and the site owner.

The other documentation that the seller must also give the person is set out in the above Buyer's Information Form and includes the agreement, site rules, evidence of charges payable for utilities and any survey of the park home.

If the current home owner acquired their park home before 26 May 2013, the purchaser and the seller will be required to send to the site owner a Notice of Proposed Sale Form containing the name and, if the site has rules, confirmation that they will comply with any site rules concerning age restrictions, the keeping of pets and the parking of vehicles.

The sale can go ahead if the seller does not receive a notification within 21 days of the service of the Notice of Proposed Sale Form that the site owner has applied to a tribunal for a Refusal Order on the grounds that the purchaser will not comply with these rules, or there is insufficient evidence of compliance. The seller will have to transfer the pitch agreement (this is called the Assignment) to the purchaser. Both seller and purchaser will need to complete an Assignment Form which provides confirmation of the agreed purchase price, the commission payable to the site owner and the pitch fee payable by the new occupier.

The purchaser will be required to provide the site owner with details of the seller's forwarding address when they notify the site owner that they are the new owner of the home. The purchaser must therefore ensure that the seller provides them with a forwarding address.

The purchaser will need to retain 10% of the purchase price to pay to the site owner, although this does not become payable until the site owner has provided his bank details following the service of the Notice of Assignment (see below).

There will be no need to inform the site owner of the sale where the home was acquired by the seller after 26 May 2013. Within seven days of the assignment, the purchaser must complete and send a Notice of Assignment form to the site owner with documentary evidence of the price paid for the park home.

As soon as is practicable after receipt of the Notice of Assignment, the site owner must provide the purchaser with details of their bank account into which the commission should be paid. The payment of the commission does not become due until the site owner has provided the purchaser with his bank details. On receipt of the details, the purchaser will have seven days to pay the commission into the site owner's bank account.

Gifting a park home to family member

The Mobile Homes Act 1983 enables a park home owner to assign their agreement with the site owner to a member of their family (this is defined in the Mobile Homes Act 1983 and includes spouse, parent, child, grandparent, grandchild and brother or sister). The changes introduced by the Mobile Homes Act 2013 to the process whereby a park home in England can be gifted to a family member mirror those for the sale of a park home. This means that the site owner is not required to approve the gift and any inconsistent provision in the agreement or site rules will not be enforceable.

It should be noted that until changes are made to the law in Wales, the consent of the site owner will be required for a gift of a park home to a family member there.

The new process for receiving a gift of a park home in England

Documentation should be provided to the family member to whom it is proposed to gift the park home They should receive a copy of the agreement, site rules, evidence of the charges payable for utilities and any survey of the park home as for a normal sale (although there is no requirement for the current occupier to provide you with the Buyer's Information Form).

Informing the site owner about the gift of the home

Where the current occupier (the family member gifting the home) acquired the park home before 26 May 2013, they will need to complete and send a Notice of Proposed Gift to the site owner providing details of how a person is related to him or her, together with supporting documentary evidence such as a birth or marriage certificate.

Where there are site rules concerning the age of the occupant, the keeping of pets and the parking of vehicles, the person making the gift will need to provide information to the site owner confirming that the person to whom the home is being gifted is able to comply with these rules.

The family member gifting the park home can then proceed with the assignment provided that he has not been informed by the site owner within 21 days of the service of the Notice of Proposed Gift that an application has been made to a First-tier Tribunal (Property Chamber) for a Refusal Order, or if he has already been informed that there is no objection to the proposed gift. It should be noted that this stage will not be necessary where the home is acquired after 26 May 2013.

The family member gifting the home will have to transfer the pitch agreement (this is called the Assignment). Both gifter and the person being gifted to will need to complete and sign an Assignment Form. They must also ensure that the family member gifting the home provides a forwarding address.

The final stage is to complete a Notice of Assignment which the new owner must send to the site owner within seven days of the assignment.

No commission will be payable on the gift of a park home to a family member

Protection from eviction

The Mobile Homes Act 1983, as amended by the Housing Act 2004, gives owners the right to keep their homes on the site they occupy indefinitely. There can only be a fixed time limit on the agreement if the site owner's planning permission, or right to use the land, is itself limited to a fixed period. If the time limit is later extended, then so is your right to stay there. The resident can bring the agreement to an end by giving at least four weeks notice in writing. The site owner can only bring the agreement to an end by applying to the county court or to an arbitrator.

There are only three grounds on which the site owner can seek to end an agreement:

- a person is not living in the mobile home as your main residence.
- The mobile home is having a detrimental effect on the site because of its age or condition or is likely to have this effect within the next five years. The site owner can only try to use this ground for ending the agreement once in any five-year period, starting from the date the agreement began.

- an occupier has broken one of the terms of the agreement and the court or the arbitrator thinks it is reasonable to end the agreement. The site owner must first tell them that they have broken the agreement and give them a reasonable time to put things right.

If the site owner can prove to the court or the arbitrator that the agreement should be brought to an end for one of these reasons, the site owner can then get an eviction order from the courts. Arbitrators cannot make eviction orders. The site owner can normally go to court to end the agreement and for an eviction order at the same time.

If the site is privately owned, the court can suspend an eviction order for up to one year, but cannot suspend it if the site is owned by the local council. It is a criminal offence for the site owner to evict a person without a court order, to harass or threaten them or to cut off services such as gas, electricity or water in order to get them to leave.

The site owner can only make a occupier move to another part of the site if:

- Their agreement says that this can be done
- The new pitch is broadly comparable to the old one
- The site owner pays all the costs.

Other rights and obligations-Charges-Pitch fee

An occupier have to pay a 'pitch fee' to the park owner to rent the land their park home sits on. The park owner can propose to change it once a year. They must give you 28 days' notice in writing. The occupier or the park owner can apply to a tribunal to decide the pitch fee if they can't agree on it.

Gas, water, electricity and liquefied petroleum gas (LPG)

The Office of the Gas and Electricity Markets (Ofgem) sets the amount the park owner can charge for gas and electricity. The park owner can't charge more for gas and electricity than they paid for it, including any connection charges. For water, the park owner can only charge what the water company charges and a reasonable administration fee. Charges for LPG aren't regulated.

Park improvements

If the park owner plans to make improvements, they must:

- give at least 28 days' notice in writing and let the occupier know how they can comment on the plans
- tell them if it will affect their pitch fee

They can go ahead with improvements even if most residents disagree. The park owner can sometimes recover improvement costs through a pitch fee increase. If occupiers disagree, they can apply to a tribunal.

Residents' associations

Residents can set up a 'qualifying' residents' association to represent home owners of the mobile home park where they live. Qualifying residents' associations have certain rights and park owners should consult the residents' association when they want to spend money on improvements or change how they run the park.

Park owners must give at least 28 days' notice of any changes and take the association's concerns into account before they make changes.

Setting up a qualifying residents' association

The association must include at least half of the home owners in the park. Residents who rent their homes can't join. Residents have to keep certain records and documents, like an up-to-date list of members, a constitution, any other rules of the association.

They will have to elect a:
- chairman
- secretary
- treasurer

The chairman, secretary and treasurer can make administrative decisions. Members should vote on all other decisions. Residents need to ask the park owner to 'acknowledge' their association. They can apply to a tribunal if the owner refuses. The Tribunal can order the park owner to acknowledge the association. The association can continue to meet if it doesn't meet the qualifying conditions but the park owner won't have to talk to the association about park operations and management.

7. Settling disputes

If occupiers have a dispute with the park owner that they can't work out, they can apply to a tribunal. Decisions made by the tribunal are legally binding. The tribunal can settle certain disputes, eg:

- changing a residence agreement
- changing the pitch fee
- moving a park home
- damage and repairs to the site
- transferring ownership of a park home to someone else

Renting a park home

A person has a rent contract if they pay rent to a landlord. It doesn't have to be in writing. If they don't have a written contract they should be able to stay for a year from the date they moved in even if they don't have anything in writing.

If you have a written contract

A written contract should say how long a person can live in their home. During this time the landlord can still ask a person to leave if:

- the contract says they can ask them to leave with 4 weeks' notice
- a person breaks the rules ('terms') of the contract and it says the owner can ask them to leave as a result

When your contract ends

The landlord can ask a person to leave as long as they give 4 weeks' notice. If a person does not leave the owner can ask the court for an 'eviction order' which forces them to leave.

A person will have more rights to stay if they live on a 'protected site'. A protected site is a mobile home park which has planning permission to have residents living there throughout the year. A holiday park isn't a protected site.

The right to stay also depends on:

- what the rental contract says
- whether the home is counted as a 'dwelling house', which means they have rights arising from tenancy laws
- To be a dwelling house the park home must be:
- the permanent residence – where they live most or all of the time
- connected to mains electricity or water
- unmovable or so large that it can't be moved in one piece, eg they can't drive it or tow it away.

Types of tenancy

The type of tenancy an occupier has depends on the date they moved in and started paying rent. They will have:

- a regulated tenancy if they moved in and started paying rent before 15 January 1989

- an assured or assured shorthold tenancy if they moved in and started paying rent on or after 15 January 1989

Houseboats

Living on a houseboat may be a more affordable option than buying or renting a flat or house. This section looks at some of the issues to consider, such as how to pay for a houseboat and where to moor it. You may be able to get help from a marine finance specialist to buy a houseboat. Before you buy a houseboat, check you can moor it somewhere. You may be able to claim housing benefit to help with costs

Buying a houseboat

If you are buying a houseboat, there are a few things you should consider.

Finance

You cannot get a mortgage to buy a houseboat from a high street bank or building society. If you can't buy outright, you may have to approach a marine finance specialist who charge higher rates of interest and are unlikely to lend you more than 80 per cent of the purchase price. The repayment term is likely to be 15 years. You may not to be able to borrow to fund the purchase of a sea-faring houseboat unless the loan can be secured on a home that you already own.

Buyer beware

Houseboats do not come with title deeds in the same way that houses do. If you are planning to buy a houseboat, make sure that the seller actually owns the boat and has a legal right to sell it. If you don't check, you could lose all your money and your houseboat.

Survey

You should get a survey done by someone who is an expert in houseboats, unless you know a lot about the subject. You don't want to buy a houseboat only to discover later that you are sinking.

Houseboats don't always come with running water, electricity, gas, central heating, telephone points, an address or rubbish collection. You should consider how to access services that are essential to you. Heating is particularly important, as life on the water can be very cold.

Residential moorings for houseboats

If you plan to live on your houseboat, you need to find a residential mooring. You can rent a residential mooring from the local council or a private landlord. You'll probably need to sign a rental agreement with your landlord, giving you both certain rights and responsibilities. Make sure you read the agreement carefully first.Cruising moorings are only intended for people who are cruising the waterways. They are not intended for people to moor houseboats on a permanent basis.

If you cannot find a residential mooring for your houseboat, you can apply to the council as homeless.

Renting a houseboat

If you rent a houseboat, make sure that it is being rented to you with a residential mooring. Most residential moorings do not allow houseboats to be rented out, so make sure that your landlord has permission for you to stay there. The usual rules regarding security of tenure apply. A Citizens Advice Bureau will advise you further.

Paying council tax for a houseboat

You have to pay council tax if you live on a houseboat with a residential mooring.

Claiming housing benefit when living on a houseboat

If you live on a houseboat, you can claim housing benefit to help pay your mooring fees and rent, if you rent rather than own it.

****

11

Service Charges and the Law

By far the commonest cause of dispute between leaseholders and freeholders is the provision of services and the levying of service charges. In extreme cases, leaseholders have been asked to contribute thousands of pounds towards the cost of major repairs, and have even suffered forfeiture of the lease if they are unable, or unwilling, to comply. Happily, such instances are rare; but even where the service charges are more moderate, they are often resented by leaseholders.

The landlord of rented property is expected to meet virtually all costs from the rent, whereas the freeholder of leasehold stock has no rent to fall back on (apart from the normally negligible ground rent). How, then, are major costs to be met when they arise? The answer, of course, is from the service charge, which is, therefore, of central importance to the management of leasehold property.

From the freeholder's point of view, the logic of service charges is impeccable. It is perfectly reasonable for freeholders to point out:

- that leaseholders benefit from the work because it has maintained or improved their homes; and
- that the fact that the work has been done means that leaseholders will get a better price when they come to sell; and
- that people that own their homes freehold have to find the money to meet costs of this kind.

In short, the purchase of a lease means the acceptance of a commitment to pay the appropriate share of costs. But this does not mean that leaseholders have no scope to challenge or query service charges. Under sections 18 to 30 of the Landlord and Tenant Act 1985, as amended by the 2002 Commonhold and Leasehold Reform Act, they have extensive legal protection against improper or unreasonable charging by freeholders, and this is discussed later in the Chapter. First, however, we should look at how a typical service charge is made up.

What goes into a Service Charge?

The lease will say how often service charges are levied: typically, monthly, six-monthly or annually. It is usual to collect the ground rent at the same time, but this is usually a fairly small component of the bill. The service charge proper will normally consist of three elements.

- **The management fee** is the charge made by the freeholder, or the freeholder's agent, to cover the administrative cost of providing the service and collecting the charge. Usually it will be much the same amount from one year to the next, but if major works have occurred the management fee will usually be higher to cover the extra costs of appointing and supervising contractors; 15% of the cost of the works is a common figure.

- **Direct costs (routine expenditure)** cover costs such as the supply of electricity to communal areas, building insurance, and the like. Again, these costs are likely to be fairly constant from year to year, so leaseholders know in advance roughly how much they are likely to have to pay.

- **Direct costs (exceptional expenditure)** cover costs that are likely to be irregular but heavy. They usually result from maintenance and repair, and it is because this component of the service charge is so unpredictable that it gives rise to so many problems. Where a house has been divided into leasehold flats, the freeholder's costs will usually be similar to what a normal homeowner would be obliged to pay; in other words, the costs may well be in the thousands (for a new roof, say) but are unlikely to be higher. Even so, a charge of £5000 for a new roof, even if divided between three or four flats, is still a major cost from the point of view of the individual leaseholder, especially if it is unexpected. The situation can be far worse in blocks of flats, where the costs of essential repair and maintenance may run into millions. Replacement of worn-out lifts, for example, is notoriously costly; and costs arising from structural defects are likely to be higher still.

Unreasonable Service Charges-General Principles

Sections 18 to 30 of the Landlord and Tenant Act 1985, as amended by the Landlord and Tenant Act 1987, and the Commonhold and Leasehold Reform Act 2002, grant substantial protection to leaseholders of residential property. This protection was introduced after complaints of exploitation by unscrupulous leaseholders, who were alleged to be carrying out unnecessary, or even fictitious, repairs at extravagant prices, whilst not providing the information that would have enabled leaseholders to query the bill. The effect of the Acts is to require freeholders to provide leaseholders with full information about service charges and to consult them before expensive works are carried out.

A few leases, namely those granted under the right to buy by local authorities or registered housing associations, have some additional protection under the Housing Act 1985 (see below), but sections 18 to 30 apply to all residential leases where the service charge depends on how much the freeholder spends. They set out the key rules that freeholders must observe in order to recover the cost, including overheads, of 'services, repairs, maintenance or insurance', as well as the freeholder's costs of management. It should be noted that failure by leaseholders to pay the service charge does not relieve the freeholder of the obligation to provide the services. The freeholder's remedy is to sue the leaseholder for the outstanding charges, or even to seek forfeiture of the lease (see below). Section 19 of the Landlord and Tenant Act 1985, as amended, provides the key protection to leaseholders by laying down that service charges are recoverable only if they are 'reasonably incurred' and if the services or works are of a reasonable standard.

This means that the charge:

o must relate to some form of 'service, repair, maintenance, or insurance' that the freeholder is required to provide under the lease;

o - must be reasonable (that is, the landlord may not recover costs incurred unnecessarily or extravagantly);

o - may cover overheads and management costs only if these too are reasonable.

In addition, the charge must normally be passed on to the leaseholders within 18 months of being incurred, and in some cases the freeholder must consult leaseholders before spending the money. These points are covered below.

The Housing Act 1996 (amended by the Commonhold and Leasehold Reform Act 2002) gave leaseholders new powers to refer service charges to the Leasehold Valuation Tribunal (LVT). LVT's have been replaced by First Tier Tribunals (introduced in July 2013)

The First Tier tribunal

Leaseholders can apply to the First-tier Tribunal (Property Chamber) to deal with disputes about service charges, repairs, extending leases or buying the freehold. This Tribunal was called the Leasehold Valuation Tribunal

What disputes the tribunal deals with

If you own a leasehold flat or house and can't resolve a dispute with your freeholder, you may be able to apply to a tribunal for a decision.

This tribunal can help with disputes over leasehold problems, such as:

- insuring the building
- the amount billed for service charges
- the quality of services such as cleaning and maintenance
- extending your lease
- buying the freehold

How to apply to the tribunal

The tribunal that deals with leaseholder disputes is called the First-tier Tribunal (Property Chamber). There are five regional tribunals. You can find details of your local tribunal from HM Courts & Tribunals Service. Apply to the tribunal using the correct form. This is available from Gov.uk.

Send the form to the regional tribunal that covers your area. The address is on the form. The tribunal contacts you to tell you if it can consider your case. You may be asked to provide more information. You can ask for a hearing or the case can be decided on the evidence you and the freeholder send. Find out more from Gov.uk about what happens at a tribunal hearing.

Costs of taking a case to the tribunal

You may have to pay a fee to apply to the tribunal. You can apply for an exemption or a reduced fee if you receive certain benefits or have a low income. If the problem affects more than one leaseholder, you can apply together and share the costs. You may have to pay a surveyor, property manager or a solicitor. In limited cases the tribunal can order the freeholder to compensate you.

If you win the case, the tribunal may be able to order the freeholder to refund your application fee. Some freeholders can include their legal costs in your service charge bill. Check your lease to see if this is allowed.

The tribunal's decision

The tribunal's decision is binding on you and the freeholder. You might need to take court action to recover any money your freeholder owes you.

What the tribunal can decide

Disputes about service charges

The tribunal can consider if a service charge is payable, and if so how much you must pay.

Disputes about repairs

The tribunal can change what your lease says about maintenance and repairs if what's said is unclear or doesn't cover the issue in dispute.

Disputes about poor management

The tribunal can appoint a new manager if you can prove your building is being badly managed. The freeholder would still own the property but would lose the right to manage it.

Lease extension disputes

The tribunal can set a price for extending your lease or buying the freehold if you and the freeholder haven't been able to agree.

Appeals against the tribunal's decision

You may be able to appeal against the tribunal's decision. You can usually only do this if the tribunal has acted unfairly or didn't follow the correct procedures. You can't appeal because you don't like the tribunal's decision.

Service Charge demands

Section 153 of the 2002 Commonhold and Leasehold Reform Act states that all demands for service charges must be accompanied by a summary of leaseholders rights and obligations. Accordingly, a leaseholder can withhold payment of charges if such a summary is not contained with a demand. Where a tenant withholds charges under section 153, the sections of a lease pertaining to payment of charges will not apply for the period for which the charge is withheld.

Sample summary of rights and obligations

Service Charges - Summary of tenants' rights and obligations

1. This summary, which briefly sets out your rights and obligations in relation to variable service charges, must by law accompany a demand for service charges. Unless a summary is sent to you with a demand, you may withhold the service charge. The summary does not give a full interpretation of the law and if you are in any doubt about your rights and obligations you should seek independent advice.
2. Your lease sets out your obligations to pay service charges to your landlord in addition to your rent. Service charges are amounts payable for services, repairs, maintenance,

improvements, insurance or the landlord's costs of management, to the extent that the costs have been reasonably incurred.

3. You have the right to ask a First Tier Tribunal to determine whether you are liable to pay service charges for services, repairs, maintenance, improvements, insurance or management. You may make a request before or after you have paid the service charge. If the tribunal determines that the service charge is payable, the tribunal may also determine-

   o who should pay the service charge and who it should be paid to;
   o the amount;
   o the date it should be paid by; and
   o how it should be paid.

However, you do not have these rights where-

   o a matter has been agreed or admitted by you;
   o a matter has already been, or is to be, referred to arbitration or has been determined by arbitration and you agreed to go to arbitration after the disagreement about the service charge or costs arose; or a matter has been decided by a court.

4. If your lease allows your landlord to recover costs incurred or that may be incurred in legal proceedings as service charges, you may ask the court or tribunal, before which those proceedings were brought, to rule that your landlord may not do so.

5. Where you seek a determination from a First Tier tribunal, you will have to pay an application fee and, where the matter proceeds to a hearing, a hearing fee, unless you qualify for a waiver or reduction. The total fees payable will not exceed £500, but making an application may incur

additional costs, such as professional fees, which you may also have to pay.

6. A First Tier tribunal has the power to award costs, against a party to any proceedings where-

o   it dismisses a matter because it is frivolous, vexatious or an abuse of process; or

o   it considers a party has acted frivolously, vexatiously, abusively, disruptively or unreasonably.

o   The Upper Tribunal (Lands Chamber) has similar powers when hearing an appeal against a decision of a First Tier Tribunal.

7. If your landlord-

o   proposes works on a building or any other premises that will cost you or any other tenant more than £250, or

o   proposes to enter into an agreement for works or services which will last for more than 12 months and will cost you or any other tenant more than £100 in any 12 month accounting period,

then your contribution will be limited to these amounts unless your landlord has properly consulted on the proposed works or agreement or a First Tier Tribunal has agreed that consultation is not required. You have the right to apply to the First Tier tribunal to ask it to determine whether your lease should be varied on the grounds that it does not make satisfactory provision in respect of the calculation of a service charge payable under the lease.

8. You have the right to write to your landlord to request a written summary of the costs which make up the service charges. The summary must-

o   cover the last 12 month period used for making up the accounts relating to the service charge ending no later than the date of your request, where the accounts are made up for 12 month periods; or

- cover the 12 month period ending with the date of your request, where the accounts are not made up for 12 month periods.
- The summary must be given to you within 1 month of your request or 6 months of the end of the period to which the summary relates whichever is the later.

9. You have the right, within 6 months of receiving a written summary of costs, to require the landlord to provide you with reasonable facilities to inspect the accounts, receipts and other documents supporting the summary and for taking copies or extracts from them.

10. You have the right to ask an accountant or surveyor to carry out an audit of the financial management of the premises containing your dwelling, to establish the obligations of your landlord and the extent to which the service charges you pay are being used efficiently. It will depend on your circumstances whether you can exercise this right alone or only with the support of others living in the premises. You are strongly advised to seek independent advice before exercising this right.

11. Your lease may give your landlord a right of re-entry or forfeiture where you have failed to pay charges which are properly due under the lease. However, to exercise this right, the landlord must meet all the legal requirements and obtain a court order. A court order will only be granted if you have admitted you are liable to pay the amount or it is finally determined by a court, tribunal or by arbitration that the amount is due. The court has a wide discretion in granting such an order and it will take into account all the circumstances of the case.

Consultation with Leaseholders

Section 20 of the LTA 1985, which is the area of the Act dealing with the landlords obligation to consult leaseholders over both major expenditure, and also long-term agreements for the provision of services, has been substituted by section 151 of the 2002 Commonhold and Leasehold Reform Act.

Major works and long term agreements

Section 151 provides extra protection where the cost of works is more than £250 per leaseholder. Therefore, if a landlord owns a block of 20 flats and wishes to spend £8,000 on repairs, the limit above which he will have to legally consult is £5,000. Costs above this level are irrecoverable (except, sometimes, when the works are urgent) unless the freeholder has taken steps to inform and consult tenants. If the leaseholders are represented by a recognised tenants' association, i.e. formally constituted and recognised by the landlord as well as leaseholders, they must also receive copies of the consultation notices along with individual leaseholders.

In relation to long term agreements, these are agreements over 12 months. Such agreements may be those for servicing lifts. They do not include contracts of employment. The consultation limit for long term contracts is now £100 per person per annum. If the amount exceeds this then consultation must be carried out. The steps in the consultation procedure are as follows:

Landlords statement of why works are necessary. There is a requirement for the landlord to state why he considers the works or the agreement to be necessary. This is defined by a 1-month period within which the landlord must take account of all responses from leaseholders. All letters and responses have to be prepared in accordance with the requirements of the Act (2002 CLRA).

Estimates. Following this initial stage, at least two estimates must be obtained, of which at least one must be from someone wholly unconnected with the freeholder (obviously a building firm that the freeholder owns or works for is not 'wholly unconnected'; nor is the freeholder's managing agent).

Notification to leaseholders The freeholder must either display a copy of the estimates somewhere they are likely to be seen by everyone liable to pay the service charge, or (preferably) send copies to everyone liable to pay the service charge.

Consultation The notification must describe the works to be carried out and must seek comments and observations, giving a deadline for replies and an address in the UK to which they may be sent. The deadline must be at least a month after the notice was sent or displayed.

Freeholder's response The freeholder must 'have regard' to any representations received. This does not mean, of course, that the freeholder must do what the leaseholders say. It does mean, however, that the freeholder must consider any comments received, and good freeholders often demonstrate that they have done so by sending a reasoned reply.

Therefore, a consultation period will usually be a minimum of 60 days from notification to instructions to carry out works.

If a service charge is challenged in court for failure to follow these procedures, it is a defence for the freeholder to show that the works were urgent. However, the court would need to be satisfied that the urgency was genuine and that the freeholder behaved reasonably in the circumstances.

Section 151 is important because it gives the leaseholders notification of any unusual items in the offing and gives them an opportunity to raise any concerns and objections. If the leaseholder has any reservations at all, it is vital that they be put before the freeholder at this stage. It is highly unlikely, in the event of legal action later, that the court will support a leaseholder who raised no objection until the bill arrived. It is common for freeholders and their agents to fail to comply with the requirements of section 151. This comment applies not only where the freehold is owned by an individual or a relatively small organisation (where mistakes might be more understandable) but also where the freeholder is a large, well resourced body like a local authority. As a result leaseholders are often paying service charges that are not due, so all leaseholders should, before paying a service charge containing unusual items, ensure that section 151, if it applies, has been scrupulously followed. If not, they can refuse to pay.

Other Protection for Leaseholders
Grant-aided works:
If the freeholder has received a grant towards the cost of carrying out the works, the amount must be deducted from the service charge levied on leaseholders.

Late charging
Service charge bills may not normally include costs incurred more than eighteen months earlier. The freeholder may, however, notify leaseholders within the eighteen month period that they will have to pay a certain cost, and then bill them later. This might happen if, for instance, the freeholder is in dispute with a contractor about the level of a bill or the standard of work.

Pre-charging
Sometimes a lease will contain a provision allowing the freeholder to make a charge to cover future costs besides those already incurred. This practice, which is perfectly lawful in itself, may be in the interests of the leaseholders by spreading over a longer period the cost of major works. It is, however, subject to the same requirement of reasonableness.

Court costs
Section 20C of the LTA 1985, provides protection against a specific abuse of the service charge system by freeholders. Previously,

freeholders tended to regard their legal costs as part of the process of managing the housing and thus as recoverable from leaseholders. Such an attitude is not necessarily unreasonable. For example, if the freeholder is suing a builder for poor work, he is, in effect, acting on behalf of all the leaseholders and it is fair that they should pay any legal costs. But suppose the freeholder were involved in legal proceedings against one of the leaseholders: if the leaseholder lost, he would probably be ordered to pay the freeholder's costs as well as his own; but if the freeholder lost, and had to pay both his own and the leaseholder's costs, he could simply, under the previous law, recover the money as part of the management element in the service charge. This meant that the freeholder was able to pursue legal action against leaseholders without fear of heavy legal costs in the event of defeat, the very factor that deters most people from resorting to law.

To prevent this, section 20C allows leaseholders to seek an order that the freeholder's legal costs must not be counted towards service charges. Such an order is available in respect of not only court proceedings but also proceedings before a First Tier Tribunal Tribunal, the Lands Tribunal, or an arbitral tribunal. An application for an order may be made by the leaseholder concerned in the case to the court or tribunal hearing it. If the case has finished, any leaseholder may apply for an order to the Lands Tribunal if the case was heard there, to any Leasehold Tribunal if it was heard by a LT, or otherwise to the county court.

Service charges held on trust

Section 42 of the Landlord and Tenant Act 1987 (as amended by the 2002 CLRA) further strengthened the position of leaseholders by laying down that the freeholder, or the freeholder's agent, must hold service charge monies in a suitable trust fund that will ensure that the money is protected and cannot be seized by the freeholder's creditors if the freeholder goes bankrupt or into liquidation.

However, public sector freeholders, notably local authorities and registered housing associations, are exempt from this requirement.

Insurance

Usually the lease provides for the landlord to arrange the insurance of the building (not the contents) and charge the cost as a service charge. This is the normal arrangement for buildings divided into flats, since it is important that there should be one single policy covering all risks to the building as a whole. It is normally recovered as part of the service charges and therefore the cost of the insurance may be challenged before or verified by the LVT in the usual way.

Where a service charge consists of or includes an amount payable for insurance, an individual leaseholder or the secretary of a recognised tenants' association may ask the landlord for a written summary of the policy or an opportunity to inspect and take copies of the policy.

The request must be made in writing and the landlord must comply within 21 days of receiving it. Where the request is for a written summary, the summary must show:

— the sum for which the property is insured;
— the name of the insurer;
— the risks covered in the policy.

The landlord can only be required to provide the summary once in each insurance period (usually a year).

Where the request is for sight of the policy, the landlord must provide reasonable access for inspection of the policy and any other relevant documents which provide evidence of payment, including receipts, and facilities for copying them. Alternatively, the request may be for the landlord to provide the copies of the policy and specified documents himself and to send them to the leaseholder or association or arrange for them to be collected.

146

'Period of Grace'

When a dwelling is sold under the right to buy by a local authority or non-charitable housing association, the purchaser is given an estimate of service charges for the following five years. This estimate is the maximum recoverable during that time. Some purchasers under the right to buy have, however, had a very rude shock when the five year period of grace expires - see *Exceptionally High Service Charges* below.

The role of a recognised tenants' association

The tenants who are liable to pay for the provision of services may, if they wish, form a recognised tenants' association (RTA) under section 29 of the Landlord and Tenant Act 1985. Note that leaseholders count as tenants for this purpose (see Chapter One, where it explained that legally the two terms are interchangeable). If the freeholder refuses to give a notice recognising the RTA, it may apply for recognition to any member of the local Rent Assessment Committee panel.

An important benefit of having a RTA is that it has the right, at the beginning of the consultation process, to recommend persons or organisations that should be invited to submit estimates. However, the freeholder is under no obligation to accept these recommendations.

Another advantage is that the RTA can, whether the freeholder likes it or not, appoint a qualified surveyor to advise on matters relating to service charges. The surveyor has extensive rights to inspect the freeholder's documentation and take copies, and can enforce these rights in court if necessary.

Statement of accounts to leaseholders

Under section 152 of the Commonhold and Leasehold Reform Act 2002, which has substituted s.21 of the Landlord and Tenant Act 1985, a landlord must supply a statement of accounts to each tenant by who service charges are payable, in relation to each accounting period. These accounts deal with:

a.   Service charges of the tenant and the tenants of dwellings associated with his dwelling
b.   Relevant costs relating to those service charges
c.   The aggregate amount standing to the credit of the tenant and the tenants of those dwellings at the beginning and the end of the accounting period in question.

This statement of account must be supplied to the tenant not later than six months after the accounting period. A certificate of a qualified auditor must be supplied and, in addition, a summary of the rights and obligations of the tenant in relation to service charges must be supplied.

Challenging Service Charges

The Landlord and Tenant Act not only allows leaseholders to take action against unreasonable behaviour by the freeholder; it also enables them to take the initiative. This is done in two ways: by giving leaseholders rights to demand information, and by allowing them to challenge the reasonableness of the charge.

Right to require information

Leaseholders have the right to ask freeholders for a written summary of costs counting towards the service charge. This is contained within s.22 of the Landlord and Tenant Act 1985, as amended by s.154 of the Commonhold and Leasehold Reform Act 2002. Such a summary must cover either the twelve months up to the point where it was requested or, if accounts are drawn up annually, the last complete twelve-month accounting period before the request was made. It must be sent to the leaseholder within 21 days of the request or within six months of the end of the period it covers, whichever is the later. Failure to provide it without reasonable excuse is a criminal offence carrying a maximum fine of £2500.

The law lays down some minimum requirements for the summary. It must:

- cover all the costs incurred during the twelve months it covers, even if they were included in service charge bills of an earlier or later period (see above for late charging and pre-charging);
- show how the costs incurred by the freeholder are reflected in the service charges paid, or to be paid, by leaseholders;
- say whether it includes any work covered by a grant (see above);
- distinguish: (a) those costs incurred for which the freeholder was not billed during the period; (b) those for which he was billed and did not pay; (c) those for which he paid bills.

If it covers five or more dwellings, the summary must, in addition, be certified by a qualified accountant as being a fair summary, complying with the Act, and supported by appropriate documentation. The purpose of section 22, as amended, is to put leaseholders in a position to challenge their service charges. After receiving the summary, the leaseholder has six months in which to ask the freeholder to make facilities available so that he can inspect the documents supporting the summary (bills, receipts, and so on) and take copies or extracts. The freeholder must respond within a month and make the facilities available within the two months following that; the inspection itself must be free, although the freeholder can make a reasonable charge for the copies and extracts. Failure to provide these facilities, like failure to supply the summary, is punishable by a fine of up to £2500.

Very similar rules apply where the lease allows, or requires, the freeholder to take out insurance against certain contingencies, such as major repair, and to recover the premiums through the service charge. This is not unreasonable in itself and will, indeed, often be in the interests of leaseholders. The danger is, however, that the freeholder, knowing that the premiums are, in effect, being paid by someone else, has no incentive to shop around for the best deal. Section 30A of the Landlord and Tenant Act 1985 therefore lays down that leaseholders, or the secretary of the recognised tenants' association if there is one, may ask the freeholder for information about the policy. Failure to supply it, or to make facilities to inspect relevant documents available if requested to do so, is an offence incurring a fine of up to £2500.

Challenging the reasonableness of a service charge

Any leaseholder liable to pay a service charge, and for that matter any freeholder levying one, may refer the charge to a First Tier Tribunal to determine its reasonableness. This may be done at any time, even when the service in question is merely a proposal by the freeholder (for instance, for future major works).

But the FTT will not consider a service charge if:

- it has already been approved by a court; or
- if the leaseholder has agreed to refer it to arbitration; or
- if the leaseholder has agreed it.

The first of these exceptions is obvious and the second is unlikely to apply very often. The third one is the problem: leaseholders should be careful, in their dealings with freeholders, to say or do nothing that could be taken to imply that they agree with any service charge that is in any way doubtful.

The FTT will consider:

- whether the freeholder's costs of services, repairs, maintenance, insurance, or management are reasonably incurred;
- whether the services or works are of a reasonable standard; and
- whether any payment required in advance is reasonable.

The fees for application to a FTT can be obtained from the FTT and will usually change annually. Appeal against a FTT decision is not to the courts but to the Lands Tribunal.

By section 19 of the Landlord and Tenant Act 1985, any service charge deemed unreasonable by the FTT is irrecoverable by the freeholder. The determination of service charges by the FTT also plays an important part in the rules governing the use of forfeiture to recover service charges. .

Forfeiture for Unpaid Service Charges

Forfeiture was mentioned at the end of Chapter Two. Briefly, it is the right of the freeholder to take possession of the property if the leaseholder breaches the lease.

By section 81 of the Housing Act 1996, as amended by the 2002 Commonhold and Leasehold Reform Act, forfeiture for an unpaid service charge is available to the freeholder only if:

- the leaseholder has agreed the charge; or
- the charge has been upheld through arbitration or by a court or First Tier Tribunal.

Regarding the first of these, it is necessary only to reiterate the warning to leaseholders to say or do nothing that could possibly be construed as representing their agreement to any service charge about whose legitimacy they have the slightest doubt. Regarding the second, it should be noted that where the leaseholder has not agreed the service charge, court proceedings or formal arbitration are necessary before the freeholder can forfeit the lease.

Exceptionally High Service Charges

So far this Chapter has focused on service charges of normal proportions that, however unforeseen and unwelcome they may be, should be within the means of the great majority of leaseholders. A minority of leaseholders, however, face the much more serious problem of consistently very high service charges. Where the cause is sharp practice by the freeholder, or failure to observe the legal requirements, the leaseholder can look for protection to the Landlord and Tenant Act as described above. Often, however, the freeholder is not to blame: rather, the problem is that the work is genuinely necessary and unavoidably expensive. In this situation, and provided the landlord carefully follows the procedures laid down, the Landlord and Tenant Act offers no protection.

****

12

Enfranchisement and Extension of Leases

LEASEHOLD REFORM, HOUSING AND
URBAN DEVELOPMENT ACT 1993

The area of leasehold enfranchisement has attracted a plethora of media and academic interest since its formal introduction in 1967 and has been amended and expanded over the past four decades. The right of long leaseholders to buy their landlord's interest outright or acquire an extended lease term, is unique to England and Wales and, perhaps unsurprisingly, has led to a number of legal challenges over the years. Landlords and tenants alike are anxious to protect their respective property interests in a market that shows no sign of abating. Consequently, this area of the law is continually evolving.

In general terms, the legislation confers two distinct rights: to purchase the freehold, either individually in relation to leasehold houses, or collectively for a block of flats, or to seek a lease extension. Although these rights are curtailed by the statutory tests for qualification, changes to the legislation, introduced by the Commonhold and Leasehold Reform Act 2002, have made it easier than ever for leaseholders to make a claim.

The requirement that leaseholders must have occupied the property in question for a period of two years (the so-called residence requirement) has largely been swept away and replaced by a new, two year ownership test. Indeed, in the case of a collective enfranchisement, even the ownership requirement has been removed. Likewise, qualification tests based on the property's ratable values and rent have gone, with the result that higher value houses, for example, may now enfranchise.

The Collective Right to enfranchise
What is it?

This gives the right for tenants of flats acting together to purchase the freehold and any headleases of their building. In order for the building to qualify under the Act, it must:

• be an independent building or be a part of a building which is capable of independent development; and

• contain two or more flats held by qualifying tenants; and

• have at least two thirds of the flats held by qualifying tenants.

In order to be a qualifying tenant you must have a long lease which means a lease which, when originally granted, was for a term of more than 21 years. However, you must not own three or more flats in the building. You cannot be a qualifying tenant if you hold a business lease.

Notwithstanding the above, the building will not qualify if:

• it comprises four or less units and has a "resident freeholder";

• more than 25% of the internal floor space (excluding common parts) is used for non-residential purposes;

• the building is part of an operational railway.

How do I prepare for a claim?

Any qualifying tenant can give a notice to his landlord or the managing agent requiring details of the various legal interests in the block. This notice places no commitment on the tenant but the response to the notice should provide the tenant with the information necessary for him to ascertain whether the building contains a sufficient number of qualifying tenants for it to qualify.

Having established that the building qualifies, it is then advisable to ascertain whether you have a sufficient number of tenants who want to participate, both for the purpose of qualifying for enfranchisement and for the purpose of being able to finance the acquisition. In order to qualify for enfranchisement, you need to establish that the number of participating tenants comprises not less than one half of all the flats in the building. However, if there are only two flats in the building then both must participate.

When you have established that the building qualifies and that there is a sufficient number of qualifying tenants who wish to participate, then there are five further practical steps which should be taken before embarking on the enfranchisement procedure.

First, you need to establish what it is going to cost by obtaining a valuation. In simple terms, the price to be paid by the participating tenants to purchase the freehold of the building is the aggregate of:

- The building's investment value to the freeholder-the capitalised value of his ground rents and the value of his reversion (being the present freehold vacant possession value deferred for the unexpired term of the lease).

- One half of the marriage value-the increased value attributable to the freehold by virtue of the participating tenants being able to grant themselves extended leases at nil premium and a peppercorn rent. The marriage value attributable to a lease held by a participating tenant will be deemed to be nil if that lease has an unexpired term of more than 80 years at the date that the initial notice is given.

- Compensation for loss of value of other property owned by the freeholder, including development value consequent to the severance of the building from that other property.

The valuation date is the date that the claim notice is given. Value added to the flat of a participating tenant by tenant's improvements is disregarded in the valuation.

155

For the purposes of calculating price, the tenants should take the advice of a properly qualified surveyor or valuer with experience in the field of enfranchisement and knowledge of the market.

In addition to the price and the participating tenants' own legal costs and valuation fees, the claimants will be required to reimburse the freeholder his legal costs and valuation fees.

Secondly, the participators will need to establish how to finance the cost of acquisition. It may, for example, be necessary for a number of participating tenants to seek a further advance from a Building Society or Bank. In particular, the participators will want to decide who is to finance the purchase of the non-participators' flats and on what basis.

Thirdly, it will be necessary to establish what vehicle the participating tenants should use in order to buy the freehold and how they will establish and regulate the relationship between themselves. In most cases, this is likely to be through a company structure, although in some circumstances a trust might be more appropriate. It should be noted that the participating tenants do not all have to have equal shares, so that the proportion of the shareholdings will be a matter for negotiation between them.

The 2002 Act provides for collective claims to be made through the mechanism of a Right to Enfranchise (RTE) company. However those provisions have never been brought into force and it is unlikely that they will be.

Fourthly, the participating tenants should seek advice to establish whether there are tax implications to the transaction, both in relation to their individual positions and in relation to the vehicle chosen to buy the freehold.

Finally, the collective enfranchisement legislation provides no guidance or controls on the way in which the participating tenants should work together in order to acquire the freehold. Since the purchase may well involve substantial sums of money and is likely to take time to complete and, during this time, the participating tenants will be heavily reliant on each other for the performance of tasks within strict limits, it is strongly advised that, before embarking on a claim, the participating tenants should enter into a formal agreement (called a participation agreement) in order to regulate the relationship between them during the course of the claim.

How is the claim made?

It is important to be aware that most of the time limits imposed on the procedural stages of the claim are strict and a failure to do something within the required time frame can have dire consequences for the defaulter. It is therefore essential that, by the time you reach the next stage of the procedure, you are well organised and backed by expert professional advice.

The reason for this is that the next procedural step is the service by the participating tenants on the landlord of what the Act calls the initial notice – the notice which claims the right to collective enfranchisement. Costs start to run against the tenants from the time they serve the initial notice. Amongst other things this notice must specify:

* the extent of the property to be acquired – supported by a plan;
* full particulars of all the qualifying tenants in the building –
not just the participating tenants;
* the price being offered for the freehold – the offer should be genuine;
* the name and address of the nominee purchaser – the person or
company nominated by the participating tenants to conduct the
negotiations and to buy the freehold on their behalf;
* the date by which the freeholder must give his counter-notice,
being a date not less than two months from the date of the service
of the initial notice.

157

The freeholder is likely to respond with a procedural notice requiring the participating tenants to deduce title. The freeholder's valuer is also likely to inspect the building for the purpose of carrying out a valuation.

Within the period specified in the initial notice, the freeholder must serve his counter-notice. First and foremost, this must state whether or not the claim is admitted. If it is not, then the participating tenants must decide if they wish to dispute the rejection through the courts.

There are circumstances where the freeholder can resist a claim on the ground of redevelopment.

If the claim is admitted, then the counter-notice must state, amongst other things:

• which of the proposals contained in the initial notice are acceptable;
• which of the proposals contained in the initial notice are not acceptable and what are the freeholder's counter-proposals —particularly on price;
• whether the freeholder wants a leaseback on any units in the building not held by a qualifying tenant (for example, a flat subject to a short term tenancy or a commercial unit).
• compensation for loss in value of other property owned by the freeholder, including development value consequent to sale

Disputes
If any terms of acquisition (including the price) remain in dispute after two months following the date of the counter-notice, then either party can apply to the leasehold valuation tribunal for the matter in dispute to be determined.

This application must be made within six months following the date of the counter-notice or the claim is lost. Most claims are settled by negotiation. If a First Tier Tribunal is required to make a determination, then there is a right to appeal that decision to the Lands Tribunal if permission is given to do so.

Completion

Once the terms of acquisition have been agreed or determined by the FTT tribunal, then the matter reverts to a conveyancing transaction with the parties entering into a sale contract on the terms agreed or determined and thence to completion.

If the matter proceeds to completion, then the participating tenants, through their nominee purchaser, will become the freeholder of the building, subject to the various flat leases. In effect, the participating tenants will replace the existing freeholder. This will put them in a position to grant themselves extended leases.

There may be taxation consequences on granting an extended lease, particularly for second home owners. There will also be responsibilities. The participating tenants will become responsible for the management of the building and the administration of the service charge account in accordance with the covenants in the original leases.

If the nominee purchaser is a company, all participators will be shareholders and some will be officers of that company. These are all matters on which clear professional advice will be needed. It is important to note that an individual tenant has no right to become a participating tenant – even if he is a qualifying tenant. It is a matter for the tenants to resolve between themselves. You can always ask to be allowed to join in, but you will have no remedy if refused. If a group does form without you – and does not need you – you may well find yourself left out.

However, if you are left out, that need not necessarily be the end of the road. This is because of the second major innovation that was introduced by the 1993 Act – the individual right to acquire a new lease.

The individual right to extend leases
What is it?

The individual right to a statutory lease extension applies to all qualifying tenants of flats. The condition is that you must be the tenant of a flat which you hold on a long lease (i.e. a lease for an original term in excess of 21 years). Furthermore, you must have owned the lease for at least two years before the date of the claim. For the purpose of the lease extension, There is no limit to the number of flats you may own in the building and you may extend any or all of them provided that the conditions are met. However, you cannot be a qualifying tenant if you hold a business lease.

Prior to the 2002 Act, the personal representatives of a deceased tenant had no rights to make a claim, even where the deceased tenant was able to fulfil the qualifying conditions. However, such personal representatives can now make a claim provided that the right is exercised within a period of two years from the date of grant of probate.

What do I get?

If you qualify, then you will be entitled to acquire a new extended lease in substitution for your existing lease. This extended lease will be for a term expiring 90 years after the end of the current lease and will reserve a peppercorn rent throughout the term.

Broadly, the lease will otherwise be on the same terms as the existing lease but the landlord will have certain additional redevelopment rights, exercisable within 12 months before the expiration of the current lease term and within 5 years before the expiration of the extended lease.

The price

The price to be paid for the new lease will be the aggregate of:

160

• the diminution in value of the landlord's interest in the flat, consequent on the grant of the extended lease; being the capitalised value of the landlord's ground rent and the value of his reversion (being the present near-freehold vacant possession value deferred for the unexpired lease term);

• 50% of the marriage value (the additional value released by the tenant's ability to merge the extended lease with the existing lease) must be paid to the landlord although the marriage value will be deemed to be nil if the existing lease has an unexpired term of more than 80 years at the date of the claim;

• compensation for loss in value of other property owned by the freeholder, including development value, consequent on the grant of the new lease

The valuation date is the date of the claim notice. In addition to the price and the tenant's own legal costs and valuation fees, you will also be required to reimburse the freeholder his legal costs and valuation fees.

How do I claim?

The procedure to be followed is very similar to that for collective enfranchisement. It is therefore important to be aware that most of the time limits imposed on the procedural stages of the claim are strict and a failure to do something within the required time frame can have dire consequences for the defaulter.

The qualifying tenant can serve a preliminary notice to obtain information. Thereafter, he serves his notice of claim (in this case called the tenant's notice of claim) which amongst other things needs to state:

• a description of the flat — but not necessarily with a plan;

• sufficient particulars to establish that the lease qualifies;

• the premium being offered — it must be a bona fide offer;

• the terms of the new lease;

• the date by which the landlord must give the counter-notice, being a date not less than two months from the date of service of the tenant's notice.

The landlord is likely to respond with a procedural notice requiring payment of a deposit (equal to 10% of the premium being offered) and asking the tenant to deduce title. The landlord's valuer is also likely to inspect the flat for the purpose of carrying out a valuation.

Within the period specified in the tenant's notice, the landlord must serve his counter-notice. First and foremost, this must state whether or not the claim is admitted. If it is not, then the tenant must decide if he wishes to dispute the rejection through the courts. However, unlike a collective enfranchisement claim where the nominee purchaser makes the application to the court in these circumstances, in the case of the statutory lease extension, it is the landlord who makes the application if he has refused the claim.

Enfranchisement

There are circumstances where the landlord can resist a claim on the ground of redevelopment. If the claim is admitted, then the counter-notice must state, amongst other things:

• which of the proposals contained in the tenant's notice are acceptable;

• which of the proposals contained in the tenant's notice are not acceptable and what are the landlord's counter-proposals — particularly the premium.

162

Disputes

If either the terms of the lease or the premium remain in dispute after two months following the date of the counter-notice, then either party can apply to the leasehold valuation tribunal for the matter in dispute to be determined.

This application must be made within six months following the date of the counter-notice or the claim is lost. Most claims are settled by negotiation. If a First Tier Tribunal is required to make a determination, then there is a right to appeal that decision to the Lands Tribunal if permission is given to do so

Completion

Once the terms of the lease and the premium have been agreed or determined by the FTT then the matter reverts to a conveyancing transaction with the parties proceeding to completion of the new lease. The tenant can withdraw at any time and there are provisions for the tenant's notice to be considered withdrawn if certain strict time limits are not met by the tenant. As in collective enfranchisement, the tenant is on risk as to costs as from the date of his tenant's notice so it is essential to be prepared and to be properly advised before starting down the road to an extension.

A tenant's notice is capable of being assigned but only in conjunction with a contemporaneous assignment of the lease. It is common for a seller to serve a notice and then sell that notice with the lease to a purchaser, who will take over the claim.

There is no limit to the number of times that a tenant can exercise this right – so long as he is prepared to pay the costs for doing so.

Enfranchisement of Houses-Leasehold Reform Act 1967-What is the right?

The Leasehold Reform Act 1967 gives the tenant of a leasehold house who fulfils certain rules of qualification the right to acquire the freehold and any intermediate leases.

How do I qualify?

In looking at the rules of qualification under the 1967 Act, there are three basic questions that need to be answered. First, does the building qualify. Secondly, does the lease qualify. Thirdly, does the tenant qualify. In order for the building to qualify, it must be a 'house'. This has developed a wide definition and can mean a shop with a flat above, or a building converted to flats. However, one essential feature is that there must be no material over or under-hang with an adjoining building (if there is, then it is likely to be a flat).

The lease must comprise the whole of the house and it must be a long tenancy, i.e., a lease with an original term of more than 21 years. However, if it is a business tenancy, then it will not qualify if it is for an original term of 35 years or less.

The tenant must have owned the lease of the house for a period of at least two years before the date of the claim. Prior to the 2002 Act, it was also necessary for the tenant to occupy the house as his only or main residence for a three year period. The residence test has now been abolished save in limited circumstances.

If a house is mixed use so that there is a business tenancy (for example a building comprising a shop with a flat above) or if the house includes a flat which is subject to a qualifying lease under the 1993 Act (see above), then the tenant is still required to fulfil a residence test. However, it is modified so that the tenant has to occupy the house as his only or main residence only for two years or periods amounting in aggregate to two years in the preceding ten years.

Prior to the 2002 Act, the personal representatives of a deceased tenant had no right to make a claim., even where the deceased tenant was able to fulfill the qualifying conditions. However, such personal representatives can now make a claim provided that the right is exercised within a period of two years from the date of grant of probate.

The Price

The 1967 Act has three different valuation methods. In every case, the valuation date is the date of the claim.

If the house qualified pre-1933 (i.e. by not needing to rely on amendments made to the financial limits and/or low rent conditions by either the 1933 Act, the 1996 Act or the 2002 Act) and had a ratable value of less than £1,000 (£500 outside the Greater London Area) on 31st March 1990 then the valuation is under section 9(1). This section expressly excludes any marriage value and restricts the value to a proportion of the site value.

If the house qualifies pre-1933 but did not have a ratable value of less than £1,000 (£500 outside the Greater London Area) on 31st March 1990, the valuation is under section 9 (1A). The valuation elements here are:

- The capitalised value of the landlords ground rent and the value of his reversion (being the present freehold vacant possession value deferred for the unexpired lease term; and
- 50% of the marriage value (the additional value released by the tenants ability to merge the freehold and leasehold interests) must be to the landlord although the marriage value will be

deemed to be nil if the lease has an unexpired term of more than 80 years at the date of the claim.

If the house qualifies post-1933 (i.e. the claimant needs to rely on amendments made to the financial limits/low rent conditions by either the 1933 Act or the 2002 Act) then the valuation is under section 9 (1C). This is broadly the same as section 9(1A) valuation except that the freeholder can be compensated for loss in value of other property owned by him, including development value, consequent on the severance of the house from the other property.

How do I claim?

The procedure for a claim is relatively straightforward. The tenant serves his notice of claim, which is in prescribed form and needs to state (inter alia):

- • a description of the house – but not necessarily with a plan;
- • particulars to establish that the lease and tenant qualify;
- • what the tenant thinks is the basis of valuation.

In addition to the price and the tenant's own legal costs and valuation fees, he will be required to reimburse the freeholder his legal costs and valuations fees. The landlord is likely to respond with a procedural notice requiring payment of a deposit (equal to three times the rent payable under the lease) and asking the tenant to deduce title and (if a residence test is relevant) to produce evidence by statutory declaration that he fulfils the residence condition.

The landlord's valuer is also likely to inspect the house for the purpose of carrying out a valuation. The Act requires the landlord to state, within two months of the notice of claim being served, whether or not he admits the claim. If the claim is not admitted then the tenant must decide if he wishes to dispute the rejection through the courts. A freeholder cannot resist a claim on redevelopment grounds.

Disputes.

If the claim is admitted and either the terms of the conveyance or the price remain in dispute after two months following the date of the notice of claim, then either party can apply to the leasehold valuation tribunal for the matter in dispute to be determined. There are no time limits on the making of this application.

Completion

Once the terms of the conveyance and the purchase price have been agreed or determined by the leasehold valuation tribunal, the matter reverts to a conveyancing transaction with the parties proceeding to completion.

The tenant can withdraw at any time up to one month following the determination of the purchase price. Unlike collective enfranchisement and statutory lease extension claims, there are no strict procedural time limits. However, the tenant is liable for the landlord's costs as from the date of his notice of claim.

The extended lease option

The 1967 Act also allows the qualifying tenant of a house to take an extended lease of the house for a term of 50 years to expire after the term date of the existing lease at a modern ground rent throughout the extended term and without payment of a premium. This right has been little exercised in recent years not least because none of the amendments relating to the abolition of financial limits and the low rent test introduced by the 1993 Act, the 1996 Act and the 2002 Act apply to it.

Furthermore, the extended lease originally had no statutory protection and carried no right to acquire the freehold.

However, following the 2002 Act, all tenancies extended under the 1967 Act now have security of tenure. Furthermore, the tenant under an extended lease now has the right to acquire the freehold, if he otherwise fulfils the qualifying conditions; in such cases, the purchase price will be determined in accordance with section 9(1C) but with modified assumptions.

****

13

Business Tenancies

Business tenancies

A business tenancy is the same as any other tenancy with the exception that it is governed by the Landlord and Tenant Act 1954. To be eligible for protection as a business tenant the occupier must fall within the definition provided by section 23 of the 1954 Act which states:

1) Subject to the provisions of this Act, this part of the Act applies to any tenancy where the property comprised in the tenancy is or includes premises which are occupied by the tenant and are so occupied for the purposes of a business carried on by him or for those and other purposes.

A person will be a business tenant if he or she has a tenancy of that premises, occupies a part of the premises and the premises are occupied solely for the purposes of carrying on a business.

A business tenancy may be periodic or fixed term. A sub-tenant will also be protected. However, a licence to occupy will not be protected under the 1954 Act. The principles of Street v Mountford will apply with business tenancies. By merely wording what is in reality a tenancy a licence, the landlord cannot escape the provisions of the 1954 Act. However, it was highlighted in the case Dresden Estates Ltd v Collinson (1987) 1 EGLR 45 that 'the attributes of a residential premises and a business premises are often quite different' and that 'the indicia, which may make it more apparent in the case of a residential occupier that he is in fact a tenant may be less applicable or be less likely to have that effect in the case of some business tenancies'. In this case, the landlord retained the right to move the tenant to a different premises. This was held to be inconsistent with the right of exclusive possession and therefore inconsistent with the existence of a tenancy.

Business premises

The word premises, to describe business premises, is used in a wider sense. For example, a piece of land leased for training horses has been construed as a business premises (Bracey v Read 1963 CH 88).

Occupation for the purposes of a business

A tenant must occupy a property or part of a property to gain protection under the 1954 Act. In addition the tenant must also occupy for the purposes of a business.

Business is defined by s23(2) of the Act:

1) In this part of the Act the expression 'business' includes a trade. Profession or employment and includes any activity carried on by a body of persons, whether corporate or unincorporated.

There is a difference created here between an individual business tenant and a corporate tenant. For an individual to fall into the category of business tenant, he or she will have to carry out an activity that can be classed as a trade, profession or employment. One case highlights this Lewis v Weldcrest (1978) 3 ALL ER 1226, Mrs Lewis took in lodgers but gained no real quantifiable commercial advantage from doing so. The courts held that the facts did not amount to a trade. The whole distinction is a matter of degree, to what degree is a business being carried on?

Corporate tenant

S 23(1A) has been inserted into the 1954 Act to clarify the position where premises are occupied by a company as opposed to an individual. Under s23A occupation or the carrying on of a business:

a) by a company to which the tenant has a controlling interest; or where the tenant is a company, by a person with a controlling interest in the company shall be treated as equivalent to occupation or the carrying on of a business by a tenant.

The tenant as a body of persons

Where the above is the case the statute seems to indicate that any activity will count as business purposes. One example is where the trustees of a tennis club took the tenancy of tennis courts and a club house, the activity of the tennis club was held to be a business purpose within the 1954 Act (Addiscombe Garden estates Ltd v Crabe (1958) 1 QB 513. However, the scope of the word 'activity' should not be regarded as infinite. In Hillil Property v Naraine Pharmacy (1980) 39 P&CR 67 Megaw LJ stated:

'Though an activity is something that is not strictly a trade, a profession or employment, nevertheless to be an activity for this purpose it must be something that is correlative to the conceptions involved in these words'.

Mixed business and residential use

Statutory codes applying to business tenancies and residential tenancies are regarded as mutually exclusive. For the 1954 Act to apply the business use of a premises must be a significant purpose of the tenant's occupation of the premises. This is not always an easy question to determine. At one end of the scale is the tenant who works nine to five on the premises. On the other there are many examples in between. The doctor who runs a surgery away from home but who sees patients in his flat and the businessman who conducts an import export business from home. Both of these situations were considered in two appeals which were heard together Cheryl Investments Ltd v Saldanha and Royal Life

Savings Society v Page (1978) 1 WLR 1329 and which throw light on the legal status of mixed residential and business use.

The doctor in Royal Life Savings had his consulting rooms in Harley Street. By entering into a tenancy of the maisonette where he lived he had asked for, and been granted, by the landlord, permission to carry on his profession there. Both addresses appeared in the medical directory and both phone numbers put on stationary. However, in practice, the doctor very rarely saw patients at his maisonette. The court held that the professional use of the maisonette was incidental to the business and that the doctor has a Rent Act protected tenancy of the maisonette.

In Cheryl Investments, on the other hand the businessman had installed a telephone and installed other business equipment in his flat. The business was solely operating from these premises. The courts held that in this case the occupation of the flat was for a significant business purpose and was therefore a business tenancy.

Breach of covenant

If a business tenant is carrying on a business at a premises which is in breach of either a general covenant against business user or in breach of a covenant against use for the purposes of trade, profession or employment, then that tenancy will not normally fall within the 1954 Act. There are a number of situations, however, where it will come under the Act, even where there is a breach of covenant:

a) if the covenant extends to only part of the premises
b) if the covenant prohibits use only for a specified business
c) If the covenant allows only a specific business

A tenancy will also come under the Act if the landlord has consented to the breach.

Exclusions from the 1954 Act

Certain tenancies are expressly excluded from the 1954 Act:

a) agricultural holdings and farm tenancies

b) mining leases

c) tenancies of premises licensed to sell alcohol, not including hotels and restaurants and other premises where the sale of alcohol is not the main use of the premises, which were granted before 11th July 1989. Tenancies of premises licensed to sell alcohol granted after this date do fall within the Act,

d) service tenancies (for employment which lasts as long as the job). If the tenancy was granted after 1st October 1954, the tenancy the tenancy must have been granted in writing clearly expressing the purposes for which the tenancy was granted.

e) Short tenancies granted for a term certain and not exceeding six months unless the tenancy contains provisions for extending it beyond six months.

Contracting out of the 1954 Act

The Regulatory Reform (Business Tenancies) (England and Wales) Order 2003 inserted a new provision into the 1954 Act, being s38A which allows a landlord and tenant to enter into an agreement that the provisions relating to security of tenure will not apply to a tenancy. In order for an agreement of this kind to be valid, the landlord must serve on the tenant a notice in a prescribed form. This notice will state that the tenancy is excluded from the provisions set out in ss24-28 relating to security. The provisions of s38 will only apply to agreements entered into after 1st June 2004. For agreements entered into before this date then the parties to the tenancy must ask the courts to authorise the agreement.

Security of tenure under the 1954 Act

S24 of the LTA 1954, as amended, contains the core provisions relating to security of tenure. The basis of security is that of automatic continuation of the tenancy. A tenancy that comes under the act will not come to an end unless it is terminated in one of the ways set out in the act. S24 provides:

1) A tenancy to which this part of the Act applies shall not come to an end unless terminated in accordance with the provisions of this part of the Act and, subject to the following provisions of this Act either the tenant or the landlord under such a tenancy may apply to the court for an order for the grant of a new tenancy-

    a) if the landlord has given notice under s 25 of this Act to terminate the tenancy or

    b) if the tenant has made a request for a new tenancy in accordance with s26 of this Act.

This section has been amended by the Regulatory Reform (Business Tenancies) (England and Wales) Order 2003. Before this amendment it was only the tenant whop could make an application under s24.

Thus the method used by the LTA 1954 to provide security of tenure acts to prevent the tenancy coming to an end in the first place. The tenancy continues as it did before the end of the contractual term and remains an interest in land that can be disposed of.

Termination of a business tenancy

There are a number of methods of termination under the LTA 1954. They can be divided into two categories, the common law methods of termination which are preserved by the Act and the statutory methods of termination as provided for in the Act. For common law methods of termination the 1954 Act s24 (2) provides:

2) The last foregoing subsection shall not prevent the coming to an end of a tenancy by notice to quit given by the tenant, by surrender or forfeiture or by the forfeiture of a superior tenancy unless-

    a) in the case of a notice to quit, the notice had been given before the tenant had been in occupation in right of the tenancy for one month; or

b) in the case of an instrument of surrender, the instrument was executed before, or was executed in pursuance of an agreement made before, the tenant had been in occupation in right of the tenancy for one month.

Article 3(2) of the Regulatory Reform (Business Tenancies) (England and Wales) Order 2003 has added further provision to s24 (2) to take account of the fact that it is now possible for landlord or tenant to serve notice:

(2A) Neither the tenant nor the landlord may make an application under s 24(1) if the other has made such an application and that application has been served.

(2B) Neither the tenant nor the landlord may make such an application if the landlord has made an application under s29 (2) of this Act and the application has been served.

(2C) The landlord may not withdraw an application under s 24(1) unless the tenant consents to its withdrawal.

The aim of the 1954 Act is to protect the tenant from termination by the landlord. The tenant can still terminate the tenancy by serving a notice to quit. The tenant can also surrender the tenancy. The tenant cannot serve a notice to quit or surrender the tenancy before he or she has been in occupation for one month. The Act does not affect the landlord applying for forfeiture in the event of the tenant breaching the lease. The landlord must follow the strict provisions relating to application for forfeiture.

Statutory methods of termination

Under the 1954 Act there are four ways that a tenancy to which the act applies can be brought to an end:

a) by the landlord giving notice to terminate the tenancy under s25;

b) by the tenant making an application for a new tenancy under s26;

c) by the tenant giving notice to terminate the tenancy under s 27(2);

d) by the landlord and tenant agreeing a new tenancy under s28.

Business use ceases after the fixed terms expires

If a tenant ceases to use the premises for business purposes after the contractual term has expired and while the tenancy is being continued by s24 (1) then the tenancy ceases to be protected by the 1954 Act. The tenancy does not automatically come to an end however. Section 24(3)(a) provides that the landlord may terminate the tenancy by not less than three or not more than six months notice in writing to the tenant.

If a tenant commences business user following a notice in writing this does not affect the operation of the notice.

Competent landlord

The 1954 LTA provides a mechanism for identifying the landlord with whom the tenant should deal. This landlord is known as the 'competent' landlord. Only a competent landlord can serve a tenant a notice to terminate a tenancy under s 25 of the Act. The competent landlord is not always the immediate landlord.

Section 44(1) Of the Act provides that the competent landlord will be either:

a) the owner of the fee simple: or

b) the landlord lowest in the chain of tenancies who has a tenancy which will not come to an end within 14 months by effluxion of time, and no notice has been given which will end the tenancy within 14 months.

Agreement for a new tenancy

Section 28 of the 1954 Act provides that when a competent landlord and a tenant enter into an agreement for the grant of a tenancy at a future date and the agreement specifies the terms and date of commencement of the tenancy:

a) the current tenancy will continue until that date but no longer: and

b) the current tenancy ceases to be the one to which pt 11 pf the 1954 Act applies

Termination by the landlord

In order to terminate a tenancy to which the 1954 Act applies, the landlord must serve a notice in accordance with s25. By serving such a notice the landlord puts in motion the mechanisms of the renewal procedure. This is based on a series of time limits. The notice must be given in the prescribed form and must:

a) specify the date at which the tenancy must come to an end

b) require the tenant, within two months of giving the notice, to notify the landlord in writing, whether or not, at the date of termination, the tenant will be willing to give up the tenancy of the property

c) state whether the landlord would oppose the granting of a new tenancy

From 1st June 2004, notice should be given of Form 1 if the landlord does not oppose the grant or Form 2 if opposed, of the LTA 1954 Part 2 (Notices) Regulations 2004 (S1 2004/1005). Prior to this date the landlord may have drafted his or her own notice.

Once a valid s 25 notice has been served the landlord has no power to amend it. A notice can only be withdrawn in very limited circumstances where, within two months of serving it, a superior landlord becomes the competent landlord.

Timing of the s25 notice

The notice must be given not more than 12 or less than six months before the date of termination specified in the notice. Where a landlord wishes to terminate a business tenancy the date has to be clearly specified in the notice. How the date is calculated will depend on whether the tenancy is fixed term or periodic.

Periodic tenancies

At common law, a periodic tenancy is normally brought to an end by notice to quit. Under the 1954 Act the date of termination given in the notice must not be earlier than the earliest date upon which the tenancy could have been brought to an end at common law by a notice to quit. At common law, it is necessary that the NTQ expires on the anniversary of the tenancy. Under the 1954 Act the landlord does not have to be so precise, provide that the date of termination given by the landlord is later than the date at which the tenancy could be terminated by NTQ. The notice, however, must be given not more than 12 months or less than six months before the date of termination specified in the notice.

Fixed term tenancies

With fixed term tenancies the date of termination is easier to calculate. The earliest date of termination is the date upon which the tenancy would have come to an end by effluxion of time if it had not been continued by s24 of the LTA 1954. The earliest point at which a landlord can serve a notice under s 25 is one year before the tenancy is due to expire. In every case the landlord must give at least six months notice even once the contractual tenancy is expired and the tenancy is being continued under s 24 of the LTA 1954.

A considerable number of business tenancies, however, allow termination before the expiry of the term by incorporating a break clause into the agreement. The question here is whether the landlord has to serve two notices to terminate the tenancy, one under s25 and one which follows the contractual provisions under the break clause.

If s25 notice can be served that follows the provisions of the Act and also fulfils the criteria set out in the break clause, then this will suffice and one notice is sufficient. One case that highlighted this was Scholl Manufacturing Co Ltd v Clifton (Slim Line) Ltd (1967) 3 ALL ER 16.

In practice, a landlord will often serve two notices to safeguard the situation and ensure an effective ending.

If a landlord serves a notice that satisfies the provisions of s25 but does not satisfy the provisions of the break clause then the s25 notice will be of no effect. However, if the landlord serves a notice that satisfies the break clause but not s25 then the tenancy will come to an end. However, the tenancy continues under s24 until the landlord complies with the provisions of the Act.

Termination by the tenant

The tenant cannot end the tenancy simply by giving up possession of the property on the last day of the fixed term. Notice must be served by the tenant or obligations will continue under the agreement. If the tenant has actually quit then the tenancy ceases to be protected by the Act and the tenancy will end. However, in other circumstances procedures under the Act must be followed.

There are two ways in which a tenant can bring a business tenancy to an end under the 1954 Act:

a)   by requesting a new tenancy under s26
b)   by giving notice under s27.

The first of these options is applicable where the tenant does not wish to give up the tenancy. The second is applicable where the tenant wishes to end the tenancy. It is rarer for a tenant to request a new tenancy under s26 than it is for a landlord to apply to terminate the tenancy under s25. Until the landlord indicates that he or she wants to end the tenancy it will not usually be in the tenants interest to request a new one. The tenancy will be continued anyway under s 24 and will probably be on more favourable terms to the tenant than a new one.

On the other hand it is usually in the interests of the landlord to terminate the tenancy under s 25 even if the landlord does not want to regain possession, as it is the opportunity to grant a new tenancy on more favourable terms to the landlord.

Who can request a new tenancy?

Not every tenant can take advantage of s26 of the 1954 Act. The tenant must hold a tenancy which is either a tenancy granted for a term of years certain exceeding one year (whether or not continued by s24) or a tenancy granted for term certain and thereafter from year to year.

Neither the holder of a periodic tenancy nor a fixed term tenancy of less than one year can request a new tenancy under s 26. Periodic tenants and holders of fixed term tenancies of less than one year can still apply for a new tenancy if a landlord serves them with a section 25 notice. It should be noted that the holder of a fixed term tenancy of less than six months will be excluded from the Act by s 43(3).

There are provisions in the 1954 Act designed to prevent the operation of s26 clashing with the operation of s25 or s27. If the landlord has already served a s25 notice, the tenant cannot then request a new tenancy under s 26. Similarly, if the tenant has already served notice under s27 he or she cannot subsequently request a new tenancy under s26.

The contents of a s26 notice

The tenant's request for a new tenancy has to be served on the competent landlord. It must be set out in the prescribed form (s26 (3) and set out the tenant's proposals as to the property to be comprised in the tenancy, the rent payable and the terms of the new tenancy. A date of commencement of the new tenancy should also be specified.

From 1st June the prescribed form is Form 3 of the Landlord and Tenant Act 1954, Part 2 (Notices) Regulations 2004. Prior to this date notice should have been given on Form 8 of the Landlord and Tenant Act 1954 Pt 11 (Notices) Regulations 1983.

The date of commencement of the new tenancy must not be more than six months or less than six months after the date of the request. The date must not be earlier than that which would bring the tenancy to an end by the effluxion of time or could be brought to an end by notice to quit given by the tenant.

The effect of a s26 notice is to terminate the current tenancy immediately before the date specified in the request for a new tenancy. Section 64 of the Act provides for the interim continuation of the tenancy until the application of a new tenancy is disposed of. If the new tenancy is not taken up by the tenant s 26(2) allows for a short continuation of the interim tenancy whilst parties to the tenancy sort out their affairs.

Once a tenant has served a s26 notice it is not possible to withdraw it and serve a second request.

The timescales applicable to a s26 request are similar to a s25 notice given by a landlord. Once the landlord has received the notice he or she has two months to serve notice on the tenant that an application will be made to court to oppose the grant of a new tenancy s26 (6). There is no prescribed form for the landlords notice in opposition, but it must state on which of the grounds set out in s30 of the 1954 Act the landlord will oppose the application. If the landlord fails to serve the notice of opposition then he or she will lose the right to oppose the tenant's application for anew tenancy. They will, however, still be able to argue the terms of a new tenancy.

Termination by tenants notice under s 27

This second method of termination applies when the tenant does not wish to apply for a new tenancy. It is applicable only in the case of fixed term tenancies. S27 can only be used once the tenant has been in occupation for more than one month. Where a tenant is continuing by virtue of s24 then three months notice can be given to the landlord.

S23 of the Landlord and Tenant Act sets out rules governing service of notice. Notices must be in writing and can be served personally or sent to the last known place of abode in England or Wales of the person to be served. Place of abode also means place of business. An authorised agent can also serve notice.

It should be noted that even if a notice which is invalid because of some deficiency within, it may be deemed to be valid by virtue of being accepted by the person receiving it. Once accepted, the person waives or may waive the right to claim that the notice is invalid. Therefore, the lesson here is always read the contents of the notice. One such case that highlights this is Keepers and Governors of the Possessions Revenues and Goods of the Free Grammar School of John Lyon v Mayhew(1997) 1 EGLR 88 CA.

A tenants application for a new business tenancy

A business tenants right to apply to the courts for a new tenancy is enshrined in the 1954 Act and is one of the main purposes of the Act. A new tenancy can only be granted upon termination of the old tenancy. The right to apply for a new tenancy will only arise in two circumstances:

a) where the landlord had terminated the current tenancy by serving a s25 notice;
b) where the tenant has terminated the current tenancy by requesting a new tenancy under s26.

A business tenant will have no right to apply for a new tenancy where the tenant has chosen to relinquish his ort her tenancy by serving notice under s 27.

The 1954 Act encourages the landlord and tenant to reach agreement. By serving a notice a statutory framework is created. This framework requires the parties to set out their intentions and reasons within a time frame. If agreement is not reached within the timescales then the tenant can apply to court for the matter to be settled and the landlord can apply to the court for an interim rent to be fixed.

The courts powers to order the grant of a new tenancy or to terminate a tenancy are contained within ss 29 to 31 of the 1954 Act. Some amendments have been made to these provisions by the Regulatory Reform (Business Tenancies) (England and Wales) Order 2003. A new section 29A has been added which amends the time limits for the making of an application. Under the new provisions any application made by a tenant or landlord under s24 (1) or by a landlord under s 29(2) (for the termination of a tenancy without renewal) must be made before the end of the statutory period. This is the period ending:

a) where the landlord gives notice under s25 of the act on the date specified in the notice; and

b) Where the tenant has made a request for a new tenancy under s 26 immediately before the date specified in his request.

The time limit may be extended by agreement between the parties.

Procedure

A claim for a new tenancy should be made under the procedure set out in part 8 of the Civil Procedure Rules 1999. Such a claim is subject to the modifications introduced by pt 56(3) of the CPR. No claim made after 15th October 2002 should be made without reference to pt 56.

The landlord opposing the grant of a new tenancy

The Landlord and Tenant Act 1954 ss30 (1) provides seven grounds upon which the landlord may oppose a tenant's application for a new tenancy. If the landlord wishes to rely upon any of these grounds then he or she must state them either in the s25 notice or in the landlords counter notice to the tenant's s26 request. Once a ground has been specified this cannot be changed. If a landlord specifies a ground and subsequently sells the interest then the new landlord can only rely on the ground specified by the original landlord (Marks v British waterways Board (1963) 3 ALL ER 28 CA.

The following are the grounds:

Ground (a) – tenants failure to comply with repair obligations

The landlord must establish that the premises under the tenancy are in a state of disrepair as a result of the tenant's failure to comply with the repairing obligations under the lease. The landlord must demonstrate that the breaches are serious enough for the court not to grant a new tenancy. The court will consider the severity of the breach and also the tenant's willingness to rectify the breach, plus the tenants past conduct. A case which highlights this is Lyons V Central Commercial properties Ltd (1958) 2 ALL ER 767.

Ground (b) Tenants persistent delay in paying rent

The landlord must establish that the tenant has a history of non-payment. Occasional delays are not enough. Nor will the fact that there are currently outstanding arrears amount to persistent delay. A number of factors are taken into account including:

a) Whether the delay cause the landlord inconvenience and expense
b) Whether the tenant can offer a good explanation for the delay and show that it was exceptional
c) Whether the tenant can ensure future payment, for example by providing a deposit or by offering to pay interest in any future arrears (Rawashdeh v land (1988) 2 EGLR 109 CA.

Ground (c) – Tenants breaches of other obligations or uses of the holdings.

This ground covers breaches of obligations by the tenant other than rent or disrepair. The landlord must show that there has been a substantial breach.

Ground (d) – suitable alternative accommodation available

A court has no discretion over this ground if the landlord can demonstrate that suitable alternative accommodation at a similar term and use is available.

Ground (e) – Landlord requires whole property for subsequent letting

This comes into effect when the landlord has let premises and the tenant has sub-let part of the premises requires the whole for letting. This arises very rarely indeed.

Ground (f) – landlord intends to demolish or reconstruct the premises

This is one of the most common grounds used. A Landlord intending to rely ion this ground must demonstrate a real intention to demolish or reconstruct not just a mere desire to do so. The landlord also needs to demonstrate that he or she needs possession, legally as well as physically, to be able to reasonably carry out the works. If the landlord is able to enter and carry out the works with the tenant in-situ, under a covenant in the tenancy agreement, then the landlord will not be able to succeed under this ground. One such case demonstrating this is Heath v Drown (1973) 2 ALL ER 561.

Even where, under the terms of the current tenancy, the landlord is able to show that he or she requires possession of the holding, the landlord may still fail to succeed under ground (f). Section 31(A) of the 1954 Act, inserted by s 7(1) of the Law of Property Act 1969, provides that in two situations the court will order a new tenancy:

(a) the tenant agrees to the inclusion in the terms of the new tenancy of terms giving the landlord access and other facilities for carrying out the work intended and given that access and those facilities, the landlord could reasonably carry out the work without obtaining possession and without interfering to a substantial extent or for a substantial time with the use of the holding of the business carried ion buy the tenant or:

(b) the tenant is willing to accept a tenancy of an economically separable part of the holding and either paragraph (a) of this section is satisfied with respect to that part or possession of the remainder of the holding would be reasonably sufficient to enable the landlord to carry out the intended work.

Ground (g) – landlord intends to occupy the building

Section 30 (2) of the 1954 Act provides that a landlord cannot rely on this ground if the landlord's interest was purchased or created after the beginning of the period of five years, which ends with the termination of the current tenancy. Therefore, the landlord must have owned the interest for five years. The aim of this provision is to prevent a landlord buying an interest with the aim of going into occupation himself.

The landlord will have to establish a real intention. This is a question of fact. The landlord does not have to show that he or she intends to occupy the premises him or her self. In Parkes v Westminster Roman Catholic Diocese Trustee (1978) 36 P&CR 22 it was held that the Trustees could occupy through the agency of a parish priest. Occupation through a management company is also sufficient.

The effect of opposition

If the landlord successfully establishes any of the above grounds in s 30(1) to the satisfaction of the court then the court cannot order the grant of a new tenancy. Where a landlord seeks to rely on Ground (d) (e) or (f) (suitable alternative accommodation, uneconomic sub-tenancy, intention to demolish or reconstruct) but fails to establish the ground to the satisfaction of the court, s 31(2) offers a further chance of obtaining possession:

Section 31(2) provides that:

(2).... If the court would have been satisfied of any of these grounds if the date of termination specified in the landlords notice or, as the case may be, the date specified in the tenants request for a new tenancy as the date from which the new tenancy is to begin, had been such later date as the court may determine, being a date not more than one year later than the date so specified-

   (a) the court shall make a declaration to that effect, stating on which of the said grounds the court would have been satisfied as aforesaid but shall not make an order for the grant of a new tenancy;

(b) if, within 14 days after the making of the declaration, the tenant so requires the court shall make an order substituting the said date for the date specified in the said landlords notice or tenants request, and thereupon that notice or request shall have effect accordingly.

The tenants right to be compensated

Where a landlord opposes a tenant's application for a new tenancy under grounds (a) (b) or (c), the basis of the opposition is that the tenant has breached some part of the tenancy. In the case of ground (d) there is no loss to the tenant because suitable alternative accommodation is provided in exchange for the original tenancy. Grounds (e) (f) and (g) however, are not upon the default of the tenant but on the needs of the landlord. Section 37 of the 1954 Act (as amended) therefore gives the tenant a right to compensation where the landlord has served notice opposing the grant of a tenancy under any one of these grounds. Section 37 will apply where:

(a) the tenant has applied for a new tenancy under s 24(1) and the landlord has successfully opposed the application under (e) (f) or (g); or

(b) the landlord has specified these grounds in his or her application for the termination of a tenancy under s 29(2) and the court has been unable to grant a new tenancy by reason of any of these grounds; or

(c) the landlord has specified grounds (e) (f) or (g) in his or her notice and the tenant has either not applied for a new tenancy or has made a new application but has subsequently withdrawn it.

The amount of compensation due to a tenant is calculated by multiplying the rateable value of the holding by an appropriate multiplier. The rateable value for this purpose is the RV fixed at the time of the service of notice. The multiplier is fixed by the Secretary of State. Longer standing business will attract a higher rate of compensation.

Compensation for misrepresentation

A new s 37A has been added to the 1954 Act by the Regulatory Reform (Business Tenancies) (England and Wales) Order 2003. This section enables a tenant to claim compensation from the landlord if the tenant has not applied for a new tenancy, or has not been granted a new tenancy because the landlord has misrepresented facts to the tenant or the court, or has concealed material facts. The damages will be calculated to compensate the tenant for any loss or damage sustained because of the refusal of the grant of the new tenancy, including leaving the premises.

Where a s25 notice has been served the tenancy will continue automatically until a date three months after the application has finally been disposed of. either through conclusion of court proceedings or through withdrawal of tenant's application.

Determination of an interim rent

Between the time of serving a s25 or s 26 notice and the final grant of a tenancy, there may be considerable delay. During this time the tenant or landlord may apply for the determination of an interim rent. The application must be made within six months of the termination of the old tenancy. The provisions governing the application and determination of the interim rent are contained in the new s24A to 24D of the 1954 Act. These sections have been substituted in place of the old s 24A by Article 14 of the Regulatory Reform (Business tenancies) (England and Wales) Order 2003.

The amount of rent

In most cases, if the landlord and tenant have agreed that a new tenancy will be granted, the amount of rent payable under the new tenancy will also be the interim rent. If the landlord or tenant can show that the interim rent should be different the court can order this different rent to be paid. If the landlord and tenant have not agreed then the courts can determine an interim rent. In making the determination, the court will have regard to the rent payable under the terms of the tenancy and the rent payable under any sub-tenancy of part of the property, but otherwise the court should determine the rent as it would be under s34 (1) and (2) as if a new periodic yearly tenancy were to be granted of the whole building. The rent will be determined with regard to the current state of repair of the building, even if the repair is due to a breach of the tenancy Fawkes v Viscount Chelsea (1980) QB 441 3 ALL ER 568.

The court can, in order to soften the blow of a large rent increase due to the difference between what the tenant is currently paying and the open market rent, order a lower interim rent. The interim rent will be payable from the earliest date that could have been specified in the notice.

Where a new tenancy is granted under the 1954 Act

Terms of the new tenancy

The court will determine the terms of the new tenancy where parties are unable to come to agreement. The courts will also resolve the matter of what property is included if this cannot be agreed. Normally the new tenancy will be the holding. If the parties are unable to agree what constitutes the holding then the court will decide this by reference to circumstances existing at the date of the order. In two situations the tenancy will not be of the holding:

(a) Where the landlord has opposed the grant of a new tenancy on ground (f) and by virtue of s 31A (1) the tenant has agreed to accept a tenancy of part of the holding, in which case the court will order the grant of a tenancy on that part only.

(b) Where by virtue of s 32 (2) the landlord requires the new tenancy to be the tenancy of the whole of the property comprised in the current tenancy.

Section 32(2) is of importance to a landlord where the tenant is not occupying the whole of the premises, for example where the premises includes a flat and the tenant has sub-let the flat. Under the 1954 Act the tenant only has the right to a new tenancy of the holding, i.e. the shop. In such a situation, the landlord may have no interest in recovering only the flat and can require that all of the property comprised in the current tenancy is included in the new tenancy. Section 32(3) further provides that where the current tenancy includes rights enjoyed by the tenant in connection in connection with the holding, those rights shall be included in the new tenancy unless the parties agree to the contrary. For example, in Re No 1 Albermarle Street W1 (1959) CH 531 (1959) 1 ALL ER 250 the tenant had a right to display advertising signs on the outside of the premises under his current tenancy and this right was included in the new tenancy.

The duration of the new tenancy

If the parties to the tenancy are unable to agree the length of a new tenancy then the court will determine the length. The new tenancy can either be for a fixed term or a periodic tenancy. If fixed, then it will be for a length no longer than 14 years. The court can also take into account the relative hardship caused either party.

Rent

The most contentious area, usually, concerning business tenancies, is that of rent. When parties to a tenancy fail to reach agreement section 34 (1) of the 1954 Act provides that the rent payable under a business tenancy:

.....may be determined by the court to be that which, having regard to the terms of the tenancy (other than those relating to rent) the holding might reasonably be expected to be let in the open market to a willing lessor....

The court has wide discretion when assessing the open market rent. The court will rely on expert witnesses, such as surveyors, in most cases. If there are no recent comparables the court will look at the general increases in an area over a given period. The court will also take into account the terms of a tenancy. Where a court has to determine other terms of a tenancy then these will need to be considered before setting rent. One case that highlights this is Cardshops Ltd v Davies (1971) 2 ALL ER 721.

There are certain factors that will be ignored when setting rent:

a) Any effect on rent of the fact that the tenant or his predecessors in title have been in occupation of the holding. Time is not a determining factor.

b) Any goodwill attached to the holding by reason of the carrying on of the business of the tenant

c) Any effect on rent of an improvement. By s34 (2) the improvement must have been carried out by a person who was at that time the tenant and it must not have been carried out carried out in pursuance of an obligation to the current landlord. The improvement must have been carried out under the current tenancy or:

(1) it was completed not more than 21 years before the application for the new tenancy was made: and

(2) the holding or any part of it affected by the improvement has at all times since been comprised in tenancies to which pt11 of the 1954 Act applies: and

(3) at the termination of each of these tenancies the tenant did not quit.

By s 34(3) the court may, if it thinks fit, include a provision varying the rent. The court may therefore require a rent review clause to be included in the new tenancy.

Other terms in the tenancy

Other terms, if they cannot be agreed, can be determined by the court. In determining the terms the court shall have regard to the terms of the current tenancy and to all relevant circumstances (s35).

Where one party wishes to introduce new terms different to the existing terms in a tenancy, it is up to that person to show good reason for the change. One case that demonstrates this is O'May v City of London Real property Co Ltyd (1983) 2 AC 726. In this case the landlords wanted to introduce a term into the tenancy requiring the tenant to pay a service charge. The result of this change would be to shift the cost of repairs and maintenance onto the tenant. In return, a small reduction in rent was offered. The court held that this particular change was unjustified.

Where the court makes an order for a new tenancy the landlord and tenant are bound to accept the order, with the exception that of the parties to the tenancy both agree to ignore the order they are free to do this. Secondly, the tenant may apply to the court within 14 days of the order being made to have the order revoked s 36(2).

Compensation for improvements under the 1927 Act

Part 1 of the landlord and Tenant Act 1927 as modified by Pt 111 of the LTA 1954 contains provisions giving the tenant the right to claim compensation for certain improvements made to the premises when he or she quits the premises. The right is not very extensive and is limited to authorised improvements as specified by the Act.

The provisions of the 1927 Act apply only to holdings where the premises are held under a lease and are used wholly for trade or business and includes any under lease. Certain premises are excluded from the 1927 Act, premises let under mining lease and agricultural holdings, service tenancies if the tenancy was entered into after 1927 and is in writing, premises used to carry on a profession, where the profession is not regularly carried on at the premises and premises that are sub-let as residential flats. The following improvements are not included for the purposes of compensation:

a)   improvements made before the commencement of the Act

b)   improvements begun before 1st October 1954 and were made in pursuance of a statutory obligation

c)   improvements which tenants or successors in title were obligated to carry out in pursuance of a contract entered into for valuable consideration.

The tenant must follow a rigid procedure when carrying out the improvement and claiming compensation. The right to compensation does not arise automatically, the improvement must be authorised and pre-conditions laid out in the Act must be followed. As with all things, the whole process is notice driven.

The tenant's application should be made in the county court using CPR Pt 8 procedure. The new provisions contained in CPR Pt 56 and PD 56 set out the rules for the contents and form of the application.

Where an application is made to the court, the court must give a certificate if it is satisfied that:

a) the improvement is of such a nature as to be calculated to add to the letting value of the holding at the end of the tenancy;

b) the improvement is reasonable and suitable to the character of the holding;

c) the improvement will not diminish the value of any other property belonging to the landlord or to any superior landlord.

The court can also modify the proposed plans and specifications. The landlord can prevent a certificate being granted to the tenant if he or she offers to carry out the improvements themselves.

The amount of compensation

Section 1(1) of the 1927 Act provides that the amount of compensation shall not exceed:

a) the net addition to the value of the holding as a whole which may be determined to be a result of the improvement; or

b) the reasonable cost of carrying out the improvement at the termination of the tenancy subject to a deduction of an amount equal to the cost (if any) of putting the works constituting the improvement into a reasonable state of repair, except as so far as such cost is covered by the liability of the tenant under any covenant or agreement as to the repair of the premises.

Section 1(2) provides that in determining the amount under item (a), regard shall be had to the purposes to which it is intended that the premises shall be used after the termination of the tenancy. If it is shown that it is intended to demolish, or to make structural alterations to or to change the user of the premises, regard shall be had to the effect of these acts on the additional value attributable to the improvements, and to the length of time likely to elapse between the end of the tenancy and the demolition, alteration or change of use.

Section 2(3) provides that compensation should be reduced to take into consideration any benefits which the tenant or predecessor in title may have received from the landlord in consideration of the improvement.

Landlords can avoid the effect of the 1927 Act by putting in a covenant obliging the tenant to carry out any improvement to which the landlord agrees, putting in a covenant demanding reinstatement at the end of the tenancy and deciding to demolish or change use of the premises at the end of the tenancy. Since December 1953 it has not been possible for landlords and tenants to contract out of the provisions of the 1927 Act.

****

14

Agricultural Tenancies

If you rent agricultural land or buildings to run a farm business you may have an agricultural tenancy agreement. Every agricultural tenancy agreement is unique. We refer here to 2 types of agricultural tenancies governed by legislation:

- Farm Business Tenancies governed by the Agricultural Tenancies Act 1995 - those agreed after 1 September 1995
- 1986 Act Tenancies governed by the Agricultural Holdings Act 1986 - those agreed before 1 September 1995

Farm Business Tenancies

A tenancy is a Farm Business Tenancy if at least part of the tenanted land is farmed throughout the life of the tenancy. The tenancy must also meet one of these 2 conditions:

- if the tenancy is primarily agricultural to start with, the landlord and tenant can exchange notices before the tenancy begins confirming they intend it to remain a Farm Business Tenancy throughout - this lets tenants diversify away from agriculture where the terms of the tenancy agreement allow this
- if the landlord and tenant don't exchange notices before the tenancy begins, the tenancy business must be primarily agricultural to be considered a Farm Business Tenancy

Farm Business Tenancy rent reviews

Landlords and tenants can negotiate their own rent levels and decide whether or not they want to have rent reviews. Either the landlord or tenant can demand a rent review every 3 years by law.

However, landlords and tenants can agree on how often a rent review should take place – this agreement replaces the law. For example, you can agree on a rent review every 4 years.

You must not preclude a reduction in rent in your rent review agreements.

Farm Business Tenancy compensation

As a farm business tenant you're entitled to compensation at the end of a tenancy for:

- physical improvements you've made to a holding (provided the landlord has given consent to the improvements)
- changes that increase the value of the holding (provided they are left behind when the tenant leaves)

You can agree in writing an upper limit on the amount of compensation, usually equal to the tenant's cost in making the improvements.

Ending a Farm Business Tenancy

Landlords and tenants of a Farm Business Tenancy can end the tenancy by issuing a notice to quit. The minimum notice period to quit is 12 months

1986 Act agricultural tenancies

Agricultural tenancies agreed before 1 September 1995 are known as 1986 Act Tenancies. They're also sometimes referred to as Full Agricultural Tenancies (FATs) or Agricultural Holdings Act tenancies (AHAs).

These tenancies usually have lifetime security of tenure and those granted before 12 July 1984 also carry statutory succession rights, on death or retirement. This means a close relative of a deceased tenant can apply for succession to the tenancy within 3 months of the tenant's death.

Applying for succession stops any notice to quit given by the landlord on the tenant's death. Two tenancies by succession can be granted, so it's possible for the tenant's family to work the holding for 3 generations. Farmers with a tenancy granted before 12 July 1984 can also name an eligible successor such as a close relative who can apply to take over the holding when they retire.

1986 Act Tenancies rent reviews

The landlord or tenant has the right to a rent review 3 years after either the:

- start of a tenancy
- previous rent review

If land is added to or removed from a holding then the next rent review must be either at least 3 years from one of the following:

- the date the original tenancy began
- from the date of the previous rent review for the original tenancy

This rent review must happen even if the rent has changed to reflect changes to the amount of land on the holding.

1986 Act Tenancies compensation

Under the 1986 Act Tenancy agreements the tenant is entitled to compensation at the end of their tenancy for the following:

- major long-term improvements
- short-term improvements
- 'tenant right'

Major long-term improvements

These include:

- making or planting water meadows
- planting orchards
- erecting or altering buildings
- constructing silos, roads or bridges

- repairs to fixed equipment

Short-term improvements

These include:

- mole drainage
- protecting fruit trees against animals
- clay burning
- liming and chalking of land
- applying manure, fertiliser, soil improvers and digestate to the land (in England)

'Tenant right'

These include:

- the value of growing crops
- the costs of husbandry, such as sowing seeds and cultivations
- compensation for disturbance where a landlord terminates the tenancy with a notice to quit

The amount of compensation is measured by the increase in value to the holding made by the improvements. The landlord may also claim compensation for disrepair - usually the cost of repairing any damage.

Dispute procedures

Where a landlord or a tenant has a dispute relating to an Agricultural Tenancy (either a 1986 Act Tenancy or a Farm Business Tenancy) they can use third-party expert determination or arbitration procedures.

Arbitration is the private legal settlement of a dispute by an independent, professional arbitrator which can involve either of the following:

- a tribunal hearing where both sides present evidence and testimony
- the 2 parties agreeing to resolve the dispute using written arbitration procedures, avoiding the time and costs of a hearing

If a landlord and tenant can't agree on the appointment of an arbitrator, either of them can apply to the President of the Royal Institution of Chartered Surveyors (RICS) to make an appointment on their behalf for an arbitrator to:

- decide a rent review dispute
- resolve a dispute other than a rent review

You must pay RICS for this service – the forms explain the fees.

Contacts

Farmers can get further information on agricultural tenancy issues from the Tenant Farmers Association and the National Farmers Union. Please note that the law differs in Scotland and Wales, information on which can be obtained from these sites.

Landowners can get further information from the Country Land and Business Association.

****

Index